BO

C000177184

Welcome to Bordeaux and the Gironde!

This opening fold-out contains a general map of Bordeaux and the Gironde department to help you visualize the five large districts discussed in this guide, and four pages of valuable information, handy tips and useful addresses.

Discover Bordeaux and the Gironde through six districts and six maps

A St-Pierre / St-Éloi
B Le Triangle / Jardin Public
C Pey-Berland / Mériadeck
D Victoire / St-Michel / Ste-Croix
E The quays / Chartrons / Right bank
F The Gironde department

For each district there is a double-page of addresses (restaurants, pubs, bars, music venues and shops), followed by a fold-out map for the relevant area with the essential places to see (indicated on the map by a star ★). These places are by no means all that the city and its region have to offer, but to us they are unmissable. The grid-referencing system (**A** B2) makes it easy for you to pinpoint addresses on the map.

Transport and hotels

The last fold-out consists of a transport map and four pages of practical information that include a selection of hotels.

Thematic index

Lists all the street names, sites and addresses featured in this guide.

FRANCOIS MAURIAC BY ZADKINE

LANDMARKS

Bataille de Castillon
→ *July-Aug; www.bataillede castillon.com*
A fantastic reconstruction by 50 cavalry and 500 others of the historic battle that brought the Hundred Years' War to an end.

Lacanau Pro
→ *Three days mid-Aug; www.lacanau-pro.com*
International surfing competition.

September
Médoc Marathon
→ *One day; www.marathon dumedoc.com*
An ever-popular event (the winner is awarded his weight in bottles!).

October
Fête du Vin Nouveau et de la Brocante
→ *Fourth weekend; Rue Notre-Dame; Tel. 05 56 81 50 25*
The arrival of the new wine, and 80 stalls of antiques.

November
Novart
→ *Different city location each month; Tel. 05 56 00 66 00*
A month given over to all kinds of new performances: dance, music, cinema, theatre and the plastic arts.

Bordeaux Jazz Festival
→ *Ten days early Nov; www.bordeauxjazzfestival.com*
The best in contemporary jazz.

OPENING HOURS

Restaurants
→ *Variable, but usually noon–2.30pm, 7.30–10.30pm*

Shops
→ *Mon 2–7pm; Tue-Sat 9am-7pm; some closed all day Mon and between 1 and 2pm the rest of the week.*

Museums
→ *Daily 11am–6pm; closed Mon or Tue; some open from 2pm Sat-Sun, others all week.*

BUDGET

Accommodation
Room in city centre: €70.

Eating out
Lunch is often better value than dinner, when menu prices can double.
Entrecôte à la bordelaise: €14; half-dozen oysters: €7–14.

Going out
Coffee up at the counter: €1.40; glass of wine: from €3.50; cellar concert in the Old Town: €3–5.

EATING OUT

Specialties
'**Alose**': a migratory fish with delicate oily flesh, related to the sardine and caught in spring when they swim up the Garonne to breed.

'**Cannelé**': invented in the 18th century by sisters of the Convent of the Annonciade, a small cake flavoured with rum and vanilla, with a soft centre and crisp caramelized exterior.

PLACE DES QUINCONCES

BORDEAUX, 'PORT DE LA LUNE'

PROFILE

- Capital of the Aquitaine region; 735,000 inhab. (France's 7th largest city)
- City centre is a UNESCO World Heritage Site
- World's largest AOC vineyards (300,000 acres)
- Gironde: 10,000 wine-producing chateaux.

VIEW FROM THE TOUR PEY-BERLAND

THE THREE 'M'S

Montaigne (1533–1592)
Renaissance author much admired for his book of *Essays*, a format he may be said to have invented.
Montesquieu (1689–1755)
Political thinker, satirist (*Persian Letters*). An early opponent of slavery and a major influence on the Enlightenment.
Mauriac (1885–1970)
Novelist, journalist, poet and dramatist, winner of Nobel Prize for Literature (1952). The conflict between good and evil in human nature is a key theme in his work.

TOURIST INFO

Bordeaux Tourist Office (B D3)
→ 12, cours du 30-Juillet
Tel. 05 56 00 66 00; Mon-Sat 9am–7pm (6.30pm Nov-April); 730pm July-Aug); Sun 9.30am–6.30pm (6pm Nov-April); www.bordeaux-tourisme.com
Maison du Tourisme de la Gironde (B D4)
→ 21, cours de l'Intendance
Tel. 05 56 52 61 40; Mon-Fri 9am–6.30pm (7pm July-Aug); Sat 10am–1pm, 2–6pm (6.30pm July-Aug)

WWW.

→ bordeaux-tourisme.com
Tourist office website.
→ bordeaux.fr
The city's official website.
→ cyberbordeaux.com
Comprehensive city coverage.
→ tv7.com
Local TV station website.
Programs and online news

→ tourisme-gironde.fr
Tourist website of the Gironde department.
Cybercafé
Art Obas (A D2)
→ 7, rue Maucoudinat
Tel. 05 56 44 26 30; Mon-Sat 9am–8pm; €2.50/hr

DIARY OF EVENTS

April
Itinéraires des photographes-voyageurs
→ *Different city location each month; www.itiphoto.com*
Travel photography: amateurs and professionals, both new and established.
May
Weekend des Grands Amateurs
→ *At Hangar (warehouse) 14 and outside the city; www.ugcb.net*
Tasting of vintage wines and dinner at a chateau (Sat); local walks and visits to several chateaux (Sun).

June-August
Fête du Fleuve (river)
→ *Four days in late June (odd-numbered years), on the quays; www. bordeaux-fete-le-fleuve.com*
Fête du Vin
→ *Four days in late June (even-numbered years), on the Quinconces esplanade; www.bordeaux-fete-le-vin.com*
Two large, much anticipated events with stalls, tastings, concerts and displays, celebrating Bordeaux's river and its wine.
Vinexpo
→ *Five days in June (odd-numbered years); www.vinexpo.fr*
The most important world fair for all involved in the wine trade.
Les Épicuriales
→ *Two weeks in late June, allées de Tourny; www.epicuriales.org*
International festival of gastronomy, with stalls

from all over the world – and music too.
Musiques d'Été
→ *Two weeks early July; Grand-Théâtre, cour Mably; www.opera-bordeaux.com*
Classical concerts with an emphasis on chamber music.
Hauts de Garonne
→ *Three weeks late June-mid-July in Bassens, Cenon, Floirac and Lormont; http:// musiques.de.nuit.free.fr*
Festival of world music; concerts, dinners, workshops and debates.
Grands Crus Musicaux
→ *Ten days mid-July; www.grandscrusmusicaux.com*
Classical concerts with some of the finest chateaux as their setting.
Cinésites
→ *July-Aug; www.cinesites.tm.fr*
Movie screenings in local places of interest – chateaux, historic houses, villages etc.

Welcome to Bordeaux!

A St-Pierre / St-Éloi

B Le Triangle / Jardin Public

C Pey-Berland / Mériadeck

D Victoire / St-Michel / Ste-Croix

E The quays / Chartrons / Right bank

F Gironde

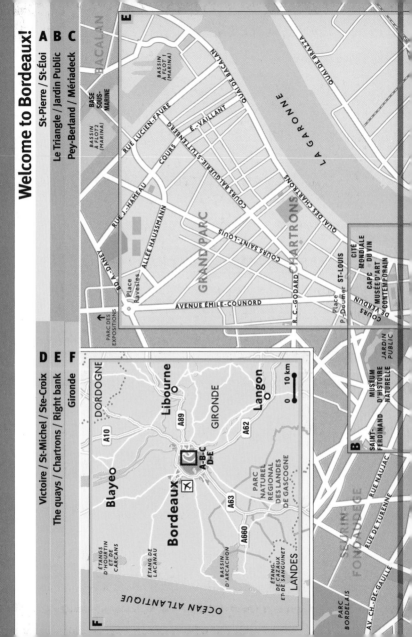

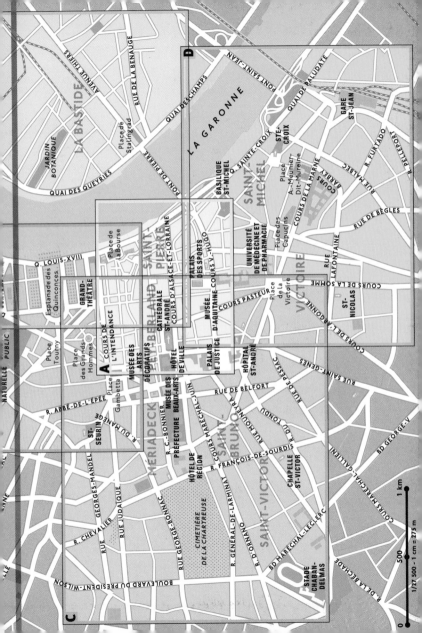

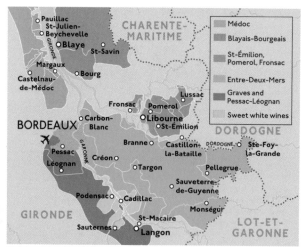

WINE-GROWING REGIONS IN THE BORDELAIS

Map legend:
- Médoc
- Blayais-Bourgeais
- St-Émilion, Pomerol, Fronsac
- Entre-Deux-Mers
- Graves and Pessac-Léognan
- Sweet white wines

CONCERTS, SHOWS

Reservations
Kiosque Culture (B D3)
→ Allées de Tourny
Tel. 05 56 79 39 56
Mon-Sat 11am–6pm
Reduced prices on day of performance.
Box Office (A C1)
→ 24, galerie Bordelaise
Tel. 05 56 48 26 26; Mon-Sat 10am–7pm (6pm Sat)
On sale at newspaper kiosks
Sud-Ouest
The main regional daily paper, with listings.
Free publications
→ In cafés, pubs etc.
'Clubs et Concerts'
→ Bi-monthly
The brand leader for 20 years, with full details.
'Spirit'
→ Monthly
Theater, exhibitions, etc.
'Happen'
→ Bi-monthly
Techno music periodical.

WHAT AND WHERE

Going out
Bordeaux has enticing outdoor cafés and bars:
St-Pierre / St-Éloi
Lots of friendly bistros, cafés and wine bars: trendy and bohemian.
St-Michel / the 'Capu' (Capucins)
Underground: the alternative scene.
La Victoire
Unsophisticated and lively: plenty of rugby fans.
The quays
The haunt of committed insomniacs, complete with jazz club and giant techno venue.
Shopping
St-Pierre
Full of smart boutiques, mind-blowing fashions, and laid-back shop assistants.
Le Triangle
Luxury goods.
City hall
Fashion designers, good

chain stores, and some real bargains too.
St-Michel / Victoire
Colorful and exotic: second-hand clothes and records.
Chartrons
Antiques on the Rue Notre-Dame.
Markets
Marché des Quais (E B3)
→ Quai des Chartrons
Sun 7am–2pm
The smartest market in town, along the quay, where you can stop and enjoy a dozen oysters at leisure.
Marché St-Michel (D C1)
→ Place Canteloup
Sat 7am–1pm
Cheap and cheerful.
Marché des Capucins (D C2)
→ Place des Capucins
Tue-Sun 6am–1pm
Fresh produce and flowers.
Bric-à-brac
Marché Saint-Michel (D C1)
→ Place Canteloup
Tue-Fri, Sun 7am–4pm
Knickknacks.

BORDEAUX WINE

Geography
Temperate climate and varied soil: dry and heavy on the left bank of the Garonne and in the Médoc, damp clay and chalk in the Libournais and Entre-Deux-Mers.
Vines
Eleven different vines (cépages), including Merlot and Cabernet Franc, soft and mellow, mostly in clay and chalk soils. Cabernet-Sauvignon, with a higher tannin content, in Graves. The luscious whites of Sauternes come predominantly from Semillon grapes.
Appellations
Fifty-seven AOC classified in six groups: Bordeaux and Bordeaux Supérieur, Médoc and Graves, St-Émilion-Pomerol-Fronsac, Côtes de Bordeaux (dry whites and sweet whites).
Some figures
■ 300,000 acres of vines, of which 95 percent are AOC.
■ 600 million liters per year
■ 10,000 growers, 130 brokers and 400 merchants are represented by the CIVB (Conseil Interprofessionnel des Vins de Bordeaux); www.vins-bordeaux.fr
Visiting chateaux
Always make an appointment in advance or the establishment may be closed. At the same time, ask for directions as it is easy to get lost, as many chateaux are not well indicated.

ST-ÉMILION

BADIE WINES, SEE B

CHÂTEAU GOMBAUDE-GUILLOT

'Grenier médocain': local *andouillette* (tripe sausage).
'Lamproie': lamprey, a slimy-looking fish containing lots of blood, whose flesh is highly prized, stewed with a red wine sauce.
'Pibale': elvers or young eels, delicious when fried.
'Tricandilles': pork tripe grilled with garlic.

What you'll eat in...

Restaurants
White meat from Aquitaine and beef from Bazas, lamb from Pauillac, snails from Caudéran, and fish (lampreys, monkfish, aloses, sturgeon and cod); as accompaniments, the region provides cep mushrooms (Bordeaux), artichokes (Macau) and asparagus (Blaye).
Thyme, shallots, bayleaf, wine and beef marrow go to make up the famous Bordelaise sauce, which is served with an *entrecôte*

(rib steak) chargrilled on vine roots for preference.
Arcachon is famous for its oysters. The Périgord and the Landes regions specialise in preserved goose and duck, and also foie gras, while from the Basque country come the black pork of Bigorre, *chipirons* (baby squid) squid and the fiery Espelette peppers;
The cooking of the region is outstanding, although today foods from all over the world are beginning to add a touch of exoticism to the local cuisine.

Brasseries
Salads, and daily menus at competitive prices, as well as more elaborate dishes: classic French cookery and local food too.

'Bistros à vins' (wine bars)
Usually low-lit rooms with rough stone walls and a great selection of regional cheeses and sausage to try

with a glass of local wine.
'Guinguettes'
Inexpensive open-air restaurants beside the Garonne or the Gironde, such as Chez Alriq and La Petite Gironde in Bordeaux, all with regional cooking.

SIGHTSEEING

Museums
Reductions
For students, unemployed and over 60s in municipal museums.
Free admission
For all at standing exhibitions in municipal museums, and first Sunday of each month in the Musée des Douanes (Customs Museum, see **E**).
Special tourist offer
→ *Contact the tourist office;*
€95–390 per person
Two nights in a double room, guided tour of the city and the vineyards, free

admission to museums, free travel on public transport and a complimentary bottle of wine.
Guided tours
→ *Contact the tourist office*
Exploring the city
General introduction, with themed walks that change every two months (famous writers, fountains etc.), and visit to a historic site (Palais Rohan, Grand Théâtre, Porte Cailhau...), boat tour of harbour, etc.
The city at work
A new way to look at Bordeaux, visiting its famous printing-house, seeing the port in operation, touring the tram maintenance sheds, and more besides.
Wine tours
→ *These are mostly on offer from mid-May to early Nov*
Visits to chateaux and tastings.

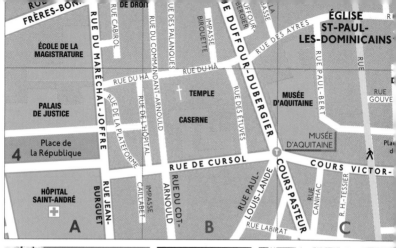

PLACE CAMILLE-JULLIAN

HÔTEL DE RAGUENEAU

QUARTIER ST-ÉLOI

★ Rue Ste-Catherine (A C1)

The longest pedestrianised street in Europe (¾ mi). Between the Place de la Comédie and that of la Victoire, it follows the route of the old Roman *cardo* (a north-south oriented street). A weekly ritual takes place here on Saturdays bringing crowds of passers-by – window-shopping! The outlines of the Gobineau House and the Porte d'Aquitaine are unmistakable at either end, while at the corner of the Rue St-Remi is the Galerie Bordelaise (1837), a covered passage decorated in extravagant 19th-century style.

★ Quartier St-Pierre (A C2)

St-Pierre, the ancient seat of power of the dukes of Aquitaine, lost its medieval wall in the 18th century, but is still very much a part of Old Bordeaux. Its 15th–18th-century facades are decorated with fine caryatids, bas-reliefs and ornamental ironwork. Behind the walls are the desirable offices of small publishers and architects, crammed between countless restaurants, fashion boutiques and other shops. If the chilly winter weather sometimes empties out the local cafés, their terraces soon fill up again in spring.

★ Place du Parlement (A D2)

Parliament Square is a classical masterpiece that was commissioned by Intendant Tourny (1775), with rusticated stone buildings pierced by large windows topped with gargoyles. At its centre stands the Second Empire fountain (1865), a popular local meeting-place with, all around, restaurant terraces that have replaced the ancient stalls of the so-called 'royal market'.

★ Place and Église St-Pierre (A D2)

→ Tel. 05 56 52 24 68 (church)
A homely little square, where local children come to play football in the sha of an ancient chestnut tre It was once the entrance the Gallo-Roman port, ar here too is the Gothic church dedicated to the patron saint of sailors an fishermen. Rebuilt in the 19th century, its light and simple façade has retaine the 15th-century porch, decorated with figures of angels and apostles. The nave and apse are also original.

★ Porte Cailhau (A E2)

→ Place du Palais
June-Sep: daily 2–7pm
Built in 1495 to the glory o Charles VIII after his victorious campaign in Ita it was the main entrance

A

QUARTIER ST-PIERRE

RUE STE-CATHERINE

PLACE DU PARLEMENT

St-Pierre / St-Éloi

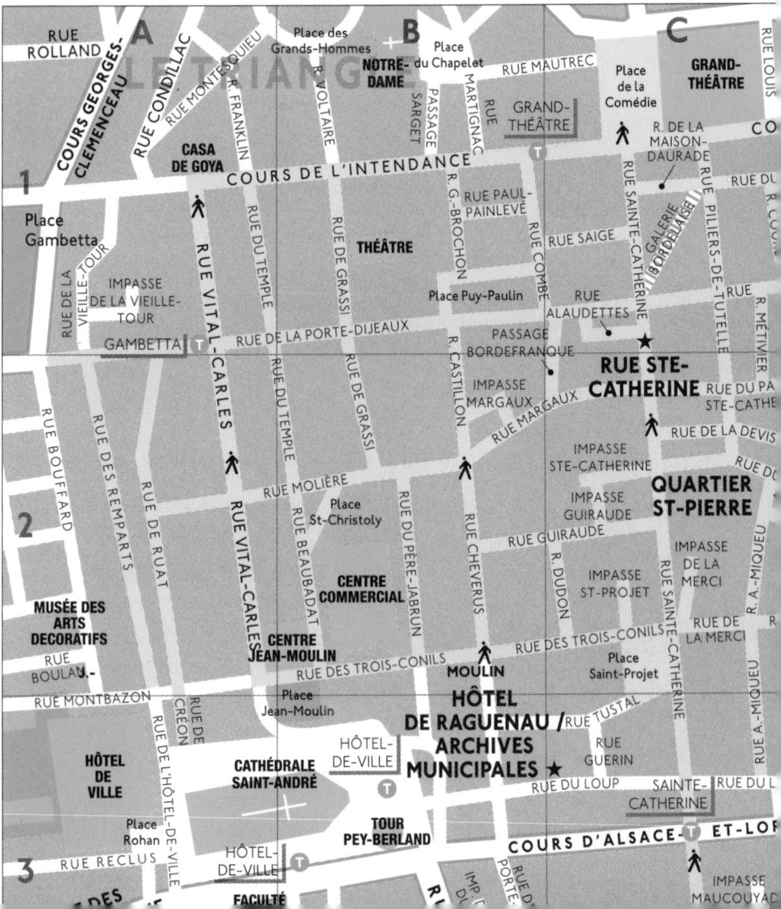

The maze of little lanes between the Cours du Chapeau-Rouge, the Cours Victor-Hugo, the Garonne and the Rue Ste-Catherine, reveals the plan of medieval Bordeaux, which was once a walled city. Now, the beautifully restored, vaulted, yellow stone buildings house smart boutiques, restaurants, cafés and wine bars. St-Pierre, which never seems to sleep, receives more and more visitors every year, but has lost none of its charm. To the south lies the much calmer district of St-Eloi. Here and there along the streets are wrought-iron gateways, bas-reliefs, views into cobbled courtyards and the unusual oasis of green (Square Vinet).

The à la carte prices given in this guide are an average for a starter, a main course and a drink.

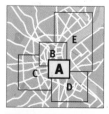

LE PETIT COMMERCE

ŒNOTRIA

RESTAURANTS

Up & Down (A D2)
→ 25, rue du Pas-St-Georges
Tel. 05 56 52 87 48; Mon-Tue noon–2pm; Wed-Fri noon–2pm, 8–11pm; Sat 8–11pm
Duck in a wok, cuttlefish à la plancha, pig's cheeks with rosemary, all served in a plainly furnished but attractive dining room. This has to be some of the best world food in Bordeaux. Daily menu €11; dishes from €13.

Sild (A D2)
→ 56, rue du Pas-St-Georges
Tel. 05 56 52 15 09; Mon-Sat noon–2pm, 7.30–10.30pm; closed Mon pm & Wed lunch
In a predominantly white decor, the Franco-Danish Sild features mainly fish dishes from the Baltic: salmon and herring, soused or smoked. Good list of both beers and wines. Menus €11.50–27.

Le Bouchon Bordelais (A C1)
→ 30, rue du Pont-de-la-Mousque; Tel. 05 56 44 33 00
Mon-Fri noon–3pm, 7–11pm
An informal cellar restaurant with ancient stone walls, and casks and bottles as decorative props. The traditional fare includes blackened Bigorre pork and grilled andouillette. Daily menu

€13; dishes €13–16.

Le Petit Commerce (A D2)
→ 22, rue du Parlement-St-Pierre; Tel. 05 56 79 76 58
Mon-Sat noon–3pm, 7–11pm; Sun 7–11pm
With their elbows on the counter, locals drink and gossip cheerfully in this no-frills fish restaurant. Sea bream, turbot, mussels or shrimps according to the day's catch, which usually counts a dozen different varieties of fish and shellfish. Carte €20–30.

Le Vieux Bordeaux (A D4)
→ 27, rue Buhan
Tel. 05 56 52 94 36; Tue-Sat noon–2pm, 8–10.15pm
Beef from Bazas or milk-fed lamb with a whiff of garlic are served in the Baroque Room or in the Petit Salon, with soil samples from the region's greatest vineyards on display. Exquisite courtyard garden, where you can eat in fine weather. Menu €19 (lunch)–39.

Œnotria (A E3)
→ 12, rue Ausone
Tel. 05 56 79 30 30; Tue-Sat 7.30–11pm; bar from 6.30pm
With golden lights aglow beneath a cream-coloured vaulted ceiling, this restaurant looks really smart. Foie gras, pigeon from the Maison Pelegris and a selection of wines

EGA-BODEGA

LE CHABROT

MOSTRA

chosen by Samuel Ingelaere, formerly head sommelier at Marc Veyrat, combine to make a feast fit for a king. Also 32 *grand cru* wines available by the glass at the bar (€4–140). Carte €35–45.

Moshi Moshi (A D3)
→ *8, place Fernand-Lafargue
Tel. 05 56 79 22 91; Daily
8–11pm (midnight Fri-Sun)*
In state-of-the-art Zen design, a Japanese eating house that has taken St-Pierre by storm. Sashimi and sushi in traditional style, or gussied up with local specialties (sushi with foie gras) for you to eat Japanese-style, or up at the bar. Carte €35–50.

WINE BARS

Le Chabrot (A E2)
→ *32, rue du Chai-des-Farines; Tel. 05 56 01 26 53
Tue-Sat 8pm–2am*
A jolly retro-style bistro filled with bric-à-brac: just the place to sit down, enjoy a good evening's conversation and try one of the 25 wines on offer, changed every month. €2–4.50 per glass, plate of charcuterie €7. Le Petit Bois, in the same street, is another, rather quieter, wine bar.

Bô Bar (A D2)
→ *8, place St-Pierre
Tel. 05 56 79 38 20
Mon 6pm–2am; Tue-Sat
noon–3pm, 6pm–2am*
From Burgundy to Spain and Hungary: over 100 wines from near and far to sample, either in the cramped little saloon or in the shady square outside. Good selection of cheese and charcuterie as well.

MOVIE THEATER, BARS, CONCERTS

Café / Cinema Utopia (A D2)
→ *5, place Camille-Jullian
Tel. 05 56 79 39 25 (café) /
05 56 52 00 03 (cinema)*
A politically active arthouse cinema inside an old Gothic church, showing avant-garde movies, animated films, documentaries etc, and with a comfortable café, in which to wait for your feature to begin.

Rue du Parlement-St-Pierre (A D2)
A narrow lane with flagstones, packed in summer when the café tables are out.

Cafecito (no. 7)
→ *Tel. 05 56 44 43 89
Tue-Sat 7pm–1.30am*
A tiny bar where you can sit and listen to jazz, blues

or electro.

Milo's (no. 21)
→ *Tel. 05 56 44 81 96
Daily 2pm–2am*
A somewhat old-fashioned bar, very popular with the locals and exceptionally friendly.

La Comtesse (no. 25)
→ *Tel. 05 56 51 03 07
Mon-Sat 6pm–2am*
With soft lighting, juke-box and an original mix of old furniture and fittings, La Comtesse is a great place for an evening out. Good snacks as well.

Rue des Piliers-de-Tutelle (A C1)
Bordeaux's Latin Quarter.

Calle Ocho (no. 24)
→ *Tel. 05 56 48 08 68
Mon-Sat 5pm–2am*
Unbeatable spot for a lively Cuban night out.

Bodega-Bodega (no. 45)
→ *Tel. 05 56 01 24 24; Mon-Sat noon–3pm, 7pm–2am*
Tapas, sangria and rioja, with Serrano hams hanging from the ceiling.

El Inca (A D3)
→ *28, rue Ste-Colombe
Tel. 06 61 56 02 23
Tue-Sun 9pm–2am;
live music from 8.30pm*
The walls shake with the noise in this very un-Incan temple, with rock, indie, punk, world and electro all sacrificed in turn on its musical altar. Pleasant

terrace for a drink in fine weather. Concerts €3–5.

SHOPPING

Docks Design (A E2)
→ *4-7, quai Richelieu
Tel. 05 56 44 54 62; Tue-Sat
10.30am–12.30pm, 2–7pm*
Lighting and unusual design furniture by the best-known names in the field, including Kartell, who has his own boutique just a short distance away.

Cousin & Compagnie (A D2)
→ *2, rue du Pas-St-Georges
Tel. 05 56 01 20 23; Mon-Sat
4–10pm, Sun 2–8pm*
A smart wine cellar belonging to Iakob Schjerfbeck, a Danish oenophile, with offerings from the New World, Spain, France and Italy. Tastings.

Mostra (A D2)
→ *4, rue du Parlement-Ste-Catherine; Tel. 05 56 51 01 03
Tue-Sat 10.30am–7pm*
Elegant vases, bowls, dishes and accessories in a range of gorgeous colours.

Michard Ardillier (A C1)
→ *10, rue Ste-Catherine
Tel. 05 56 81 86 92
Mon-Sat 10am–7pm*
A shoe boutique with a totally modern edge. A concept store, it boasts a range of famous brands, and live DJ music.

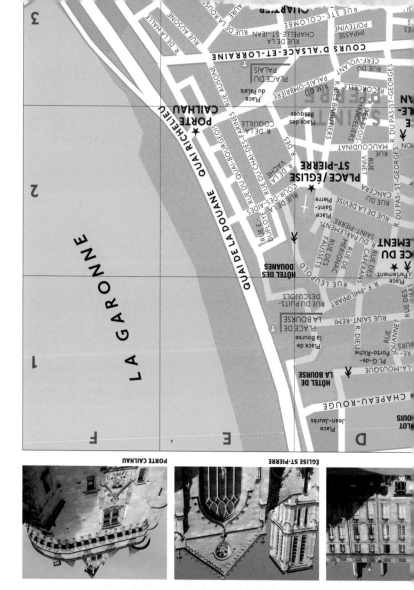

ÉGLISE ST-PIERRE

PORTE CAILHAU

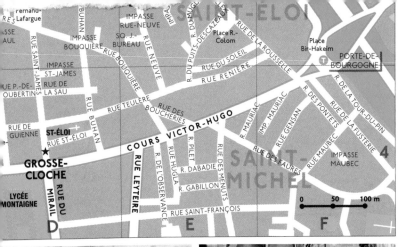

Map labels

Fernand-Lafargue · IMPASSE RUE-NEUVE · SQ. J.-BUREAU · R. DU PUITS-DESCAZEAUX · R. DU HUGO · SAINT-ÉLOI · Place R.-Colom · RUE DE LA ROUSSELLE · Place Bir-Hakeim · PORTE-DE-BOURGOGNE · BUHAN · IMPASSE BOUQUIÈRE · RUE NEUVE · RUE DU SOLEIL · RUE RENIÈRE · R. DE LA TOUR-DU-PIN · RUE SAINT-JAMES · IMPASSE ST-JAMES · RUE DE LA SAU · RUE BOUQUIÈRE · R. DES PONTETS · RUE GENSAN · R. MAURIAC · IMP. MAURIAC · RUE DE LA FUSTERIE · UE P.-DE-OUBERTIN · RUE TEULÈRE · RUE DES BOUCHERIES · RUE BUHAN · RUE DE GUIENNE · ST-ÉLOI · RUE ST-ÉLOI · COURS VICTOR-HUGO · SAINT-MICHEL · GROSSE-CLOCHE · RUE LEYTEIRE · R. DE L'OBSERVANCE · RUE HUGLA · R. PILET · R. DABADIE · R. DES MENUTS · R. GABILLON · RUE DES FAURES · RUE MAUBEC · IMPASSE MAUBEC · LYCÉE MONTAIGNE · RUE DU MIRAIL · RUE SAINT-FRANÇOIS · D · E · F · 4

0   50   100 m

...LISE ST-PAUL-LES-DOMINICAINS

GROSSE-CLOCHE

...e fortified city. Although ...st and foremost a ...fensive structure with ...rtcullis and loopholes, its ...ullioned windows, turrets ...d skylights foreshadow ...naissance taste.

Hôtel de Ragueneau / ...chives municipales ... C3)

... 71, rue du Loup ...l. 05 56 10 20 55 ...en more than the building ...self (1648) and its ...urtyard, the enclosing ...all is particularly worth a ...ok, with its beautifully ...rmed iron balustrade ...owning a stone gateway. ...e municipal archives are ...oused in the building, with ...mporary exhibitions on

the city's history.

★ Place Camille-Jullian (A D2) 'Caju' Square, named after the historian of Bordeaux (1859–1933), has been restored to life. Following major restoration work in the late 1990s, and the opening of the alternative Utopia cinema in the former Church of St Simeon (15th–16th c.), this is now one of the liveliest parts of the city.

★ Quartier St-Éloi (A D3) The medieval quarter of Bordeaux, where the city's largest market used to be held in the Place Fernand-Lafargue. Its picturesque winding lanes, in the shadow of high 17th- and

18th-century façades, recall some illustrious names: Montaigne lived in the Rue de la Rousselle (nos. 23-25), La Boétie at the corner of the Rue Gouvea, while Jeanne de Lartigue, the wife of Montesquieu, lived in the magnificent galleried Gothic mansion in the Impasse Neuve.

★ Église St-Paul-les-Dominicains (A C3) → Rue des Ayres Tel. 05 56 94 30 50 In 2006 this church, built for the Jesuits in the 17th century, was given a beautiful glass and metal chandelier, which lends a contemporary touch to its opulent 18th-century

baroque decor. Don't miss the *Apotheosis of St Francis Xavier*, a monumental white marble reredos, the work of Guillaume Coustou the Younger.

★ Grosse-Cloche (A D4) → Rue Saint-James Built in the 15th century on top of the remains of the gate of St-Eloi (13th c.), the Grosse-Cloche (great bell) is the name of the belfry of the former city hall. It became famous with the installation, in the 18th century, of a clock with a massive 17,300-lb bell– which actually once came unhooked! It now opens on to the Rue St-James and its string of small boutiques.

Map labels (top image):

au Pradeau — BASILIQUE ST-SEURIN — RUE DE LURBE — RUE G.- — RUE BUFFON — RUE — RUE CASTEJA — R. ROLLAND — PALAIS-GALLIEN — COURS G.- — RUE CONDILLAC — RUE MONTESQUIEU — É. — N — Place des Martyrs-de-la-Résistance — R. SÉGALIER — RUE CAPDEVILLE — IMPASSE ST-LAZARE — RUE FRANKLIN — RUE — RUE C.-MARIONNEAU — CAPITOLE — RUE JUDAÏQUE — RUE DU MANÈGE — RUE F.-MARIN — RUE LALIMENT — R. DU CHÂTEAU-D'EAU — R.P.-CHARRON — R. CASTELNAU-D'AUROS — COURS DE L'IN — Place Gambetta — RUE DE LA VIEILLE-TOUR — RUE VITAL-CARLES — R. DU TEMPLE — PORTE DIJEAUX — GAMBETTA — T — RUE GEORGES-BONNAC — RUE SAINT-SERNIN — RUE G.-BONNAC — RUE DES REMPARTS — RUE DE RUAT — R. — RUE G.-BONNAC — RUE R.-LATEULADE — HÔTEL DES POSTES — R. DU DR-CH.-MANCEL-PÉNARD — RUE GENSONNE — RUE BOUFFARD — R. PÈRE-DEUZAIDE — B — C

4

ALLÉES DE TOURNY / MAISON GOBINEAU

JARDIN PUBLIC

MUSÉUM D'HISTOIRE NATURI

★ **Îlot Louis (B** E3)
→ *Between Rue Louis and Place Jean-Jaurès; Hôtel Saige 25, cours du Chapeau-Rouge; Hôtel Boyer-Fonfrède corner of cours and place Jean-Jaurès*
Unity, dignity and pristine white façades: the îlot Louis (1775–78) encapsulates classical Bordeaux architecture. Designed for wealthy merchants and lawyers, patrons of the Grand Théâtre, it was built at the instigation of Victor Louis, who was also responsible for the Hôtels Saige and Boyer-Fonfrède. The latter (private property) has the most beautiful staircase in Bordeaux, which you can peek at when the door is open.

★ **Grand-Théâtre (B** E3)
→ *Place de la Comédie Tel. 05 56 00 85 95 For guided tours call the tourist office on 05 56 00 66 00*
A classical jewel, the symbol of the city and the masterpiece of Victor Louis, who went on to design the arcades of the Palais-Royal in Paris. Taking its inspiration from Greco-Roman temples, twelve Corinthian columns form a portico decorated with statues of the Nine Muses and three goddesses. The staircase served as the model for the one in the Paris Opéra Garnier. On April 7, 1780, a performance of *Athalie* inaugurated the superb blue and gold

auditorium where many of the world's greatest artists have performed.

★ **Église Notre-Dame (B** D3)
→ *Place du Chapelet Daily 9am–noon, 2–6pm*
The former chapel of the Dominican convent is a baroque masterpiece inspired by the Counter-Reformation and completed in the late 18th century. Columns, bas-reliefs and statues decorate its impressive façade, while inside, fine grillwork effectively screens off the white marble high altar (1751). Make sure to see the beautiful cloister (Cour Mably) which is reached from the outside.

★ **Cours de l'Intendance (B** D4)
With its view over the Gra Théâtre and the cours du Chapeau-Rouge, this is a splendid street along wh sleek modern trams glide indifferent to the beauty of 18th-century façades. most expensive designer boutiques are here togeth with such sights as the Atlantes on the Hotel Acquart at no. 5, or the Instituto Cervantes at no. where the painter Goya lived from 1824 until his death in 1828.

★ **Place des Grands-Hommes (B** C3.
Heading inwards from the three roads which form th Triangle are six streets

B

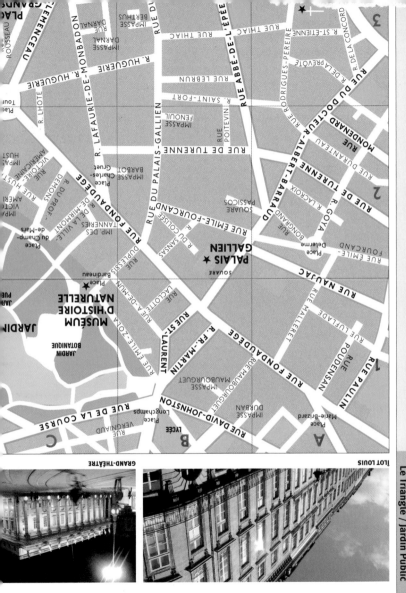

Le Triangle / Jardin Public

ÎLOT LOUIS

GRAND-THÉÂTRE

This is the Bordeaux of the Age of Enlightenment, of the great town planner-intendants and of Victor Louis's Grand Théâtre. Breaking with medieval tradition and piercing the city plan with wide right-angled arteries, Boucher and Tourny opened up the outlying districts and created the Bordeaux Triangle, bordered by the Cours de l'Intendance, now pedestrianised, the Cours Clémenceau and the Allées de Tourny. As well as an important port, it was one of France's most beautiful cities. Today, tourists and locals alike blend together happily in the smart cafés, chic boutiques and elegant restaurants of this district. To the north, off the tourist track, stand St-Seurin and the Palais Gallien.

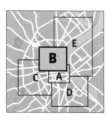

LA BOÎTE À HUÎTRES

LE GRAND THÉÂTRE

RESTAURANTS

Peppone (B C3)
→ 31, cours G.-Clémenceau
Tel. 05 56 44 91 05
Daily noon–2.15pm, 7–11pm
Peppone serves all the old Italian favourites, at their very best, and a superb specialty pizza with cep (porcini) mushrooms. The dining room is decorated with every trinket imaginable. Pizzas from €11.90; pasta €9.90.

La Boîte à Huîtres (B E4)
→ 36, cours du Chapeau-Rouge; Tel. 05 56 81 64 97
Mon 10am–3pm; Tue-Sun 10am–3pm, 6–11.30pm
Quiberons no. 4 and Clair de Marennes oysters in a cute fisherman's shed. In fine weather there are tables on the street between two 18th-century façades. Oysters €12–28 per dozen.

Noailles (B D3)
→ 12, allées de Tourny
Tel. 05 56 81 94 45
Daily noon–3pm, 7–11pm
Copper, crimson velvet, house plants, and waiters in aprons: nothing seems to have changed here since 1934, except that everything is just that little bit older. Try the sole meunière, scallops with ceps, or the braised veal. Dishes €15–25.

Le Grand Théâtre (B E3)
→ 29, rue Esprit-des-Lois
Tel. 05 56 31 30 30; Daily 11.30am–3pm, 7.30pm–1am
Bankers and celebs from the world of show-biz mingle at the bar, beneath the three plasma screens. Opinions differ about the trendy dishes cooked by Grégoire de Lépinay, but they certainly get talked about. Go for the house specials such as shepherd's pie with foie gras, or tagine of sea bream with a lemon confit. Dishes €15–30.

Café Gourmand (B C3)
→ 3, rue Buffon
Tel. 05 56 79 23 85; Tue-Sat noon–2.30pm, 7.45–10pm
A lovely dining room hung with photos and manuscripts. The menu is ambitious (lampreys à la bordelaise), somewhat exotic (wokked chicken, knuckle of sucking-pig in honey) and a bit bossy (suggesting a wine to accompany each dish). Don't miss the dessert called 'Emmène-moi au ciel' ('take me to Heaven')! Dishes €25–40.

Brasserie de l'Europe (B D3)
→ 2-5, pl. de la Comédie
Tel. 05 56 30 44 47
Daily noon–2.30pm, 7–11pm
Although it has a stunning

DES QUATRE-SŒURS

CHRIS'TEAS

L'INTENDANT

Belle Époque interior, the ultra-chic brasserie of the Hôtel Regent is relatively new. Its menu features interesting variations on classic themes, such as curried oysters, and risotto with scallops and morels. Carte €50.

Le Chapon fin (B C3)
→ 5, rue Montesquieu
Tel. 05 56 79 10 10; Tue-Sat noon-1.45pm, 8-9.45pm
Bathed in light, the fantastic rockery wall in the dining room dates back to the era of some of its most famous diners, such as Sarah Bernhardt and Toulouse-Lautrec. Today's clientele is no less sophisticated in its tastes: they love the *caviar d'Aquitaine* and roast John Dory, prepared by chef Nicolas Frion. Menu €30 (lunch), €50-78.

CAFÉ, TEAROOM, WINE BARS

Café des Quatre-Sœurs (B D3)
→ 6 bis, cours du 30-Juillet
Tel. 05 56 81 52 26
Mon-Fri 7.30am-8pm; Sat 8am-9pm; Sun 1.30-9pm
The very soul of the Triangle, with a fin-de-siècle interior. The perfect spot to read your paper, or gaze out at Bordeaux

at its Golden Age.

Chris'Teas (B D3)
→ 16, passage Sarget
Tel. 05 56 81 29 86
Tue-Sat 10.30am-7pm
A tearoom in the elegant 18th-century Sarget arcade, offering unusual and delicious blends such as Kimono, Grand Hôtel and a drink called *cacaotine*. Also rich pastries and light meals, in a setting of quiet opulence.

CIVB wine bar (B D3)
→ 3, cours du 30-Juillet
Tel. 05 56 00 43 47
Mon-Sat 11am-10pm
The wine bar of the Conseil Interprofessionel du Vin de Bordeaux had the challenge of evoking centuries of history, while being in tune with the tastes of today. It has succeeded on both counts. The 57 different appellations can be sampled from a short list of 20 different crus, which is changed every fortnight in an 18th-century setting furnished with comfortable contemporary furniture. Superb.

CINEMA, OPERA

Cinéma Jean-Vigo (B C3)
→ 6, rue Franklin
Tel. 05 56 44 35 17
An arthouse cinema

showing classic movies but also some real rarities.

Grand-Théâtre / Opéra de Bordeaux (B D3)
→ Pl. de la Comédie
Tel. 05 56 00 85 95; Mon-Sat 11am-6pm (box office)
Internationally acclaimed opera house with 120 musicians, 80 singers and dancers in the sumptuous setting of Victor Louis's Grand Théâtre.

SHOPPING

Chocolaterie Cadiot-Badie (B D3)
→ 26, allées de Tourny
Tel. 05 56 44 24 22; Mon-Sat 10am (9.15am Tue-Fri)-7pm
A chocolate shop since 1826, Cadiot-Badie sells edible treasures: gilded almonds, nougatines, Brandy truffles, tea-flavoured chocolates...

L'Intendant (B D3)
→ 2, allées de Tourny
Tel. 05 56 48 01 29
Mon-Sat 10am-7.30pm
A temple of Bordeaux wines, with more than 15,000 bottles arranged around a spiral staircase mounting several floors. The prices rise with the steps to reach the rarest vintages at the very top. Stunning.

Badie Vins (B C3)
→ 60-62, allées de Tourny

Tel. 05 56 52 23 72
Mon-Sat 9am-7.15pm
3,000 different vintages and a wide selection of spirits are on sale here.

Jean d'Alos (B C3)
→ 4, rue Montesquieu
Tel. 05 56 44 29 66; Mon 3.30-7.15pm; Tue-Sat 8.30am-12.45pm, 3.30-7.15pm
The gorgeous aroma pervades the best cheese shop in town, with produce from all over the region and beyond.

Béjottes (B C3)
→ 1, pl. des Grands-Hommes
Tel. 05 56 48 09 30; Mon-Sat 9.30am (10am Mon)-7pm
A hardware store dating back to 1830, with everything for the home and the DIY addict.

Rose (B C3)
→ 26, rue Mably; Mon 2-7pm; Tue-Wed 10.30am-1pm, 2-7pm; Thu-Sat 10.30am-7pm
For those who like to dream, or even buy, the latest fashions from Maje, Manoush, Paul & Joe Sister, Ba&sh and others.

Pierre Oteiza (B C3)
→ 77, rue Condillac
Tel. 05 56 52 38 76; Tue-Sat 10am-1pm, 2.30-7.30pm
Foie gras, confit of goose and duck, tripe, Spanish omelette, and delicious Aldude ham, which is wind-dried in the valleys of the Basque country.

LA GARONNE

3

2

1

ALL D'ORLEANS
R. CHAR...
LAF...
LAMOU...
OFFICE DE...
CRS DU
30 JUILLET
RUE
PINEAU
CRS DE TO...

QUINCONCES

ALLÉE DE MUNICH

QUAI LOUIS-XVIII

EMBARCADÈRE-
CROISIÈRES

Esplanade
des Quinconces

MONUMENT
DES GIRONDINS

Place des
Quinconces

ALLÉE DE
LOS-ANGELES

RUE DUCHE...
E DE SÉZE...
ESE DE TOURNY...
RUE DE TOURNY

RUE
BOUDET
D'ENGHIEN
DU...

RUE
D'ENGHIEN

RUE BLANC-
DUTROUILH

COURS DE
VERDUN

ALLÉE DE BRISTOL

ALLÉE DE CHARTRES

COURS MAL-FOCH

RUE GOURGUE
RUE BLANC-
DUTROUILH

RUE FOY

RUE FERRÈRE

RUE VAUBAN

RUE FERRÈRE

RUE BOUDET

JARDIN PUBLIC

Place Lainé

CAPC
MUSÉE D'ART
CONTEMPORAIN

COURS XAVIER-ARNOZAN

Rond-point du
Mal-de-Lattre-
de-Tassigny

QUAI DES CHARTRONS

CAPC

RUE FOY

RUE VAUBAN

RUE DE LA VERRERIE

COURS DE VERDUN

TEMPLE

CITÉ
MONDIALE
DU VIN

RUE NOTRE-DAME

IMPASSE
GUESTIER

RUE DUCOUVENT

RUE LATOUR

RUE CORNAC

RUE TOURAT

R. CONSTANTIN

RUE NOTRE-DAME

Place
Mitchell

RUE H.-
RODEL

RUE-E.-
GODARD

R. DU JARDIN-
PUBLIC

AVIAU

CHARTRONS

F **E** **D**

H **G**

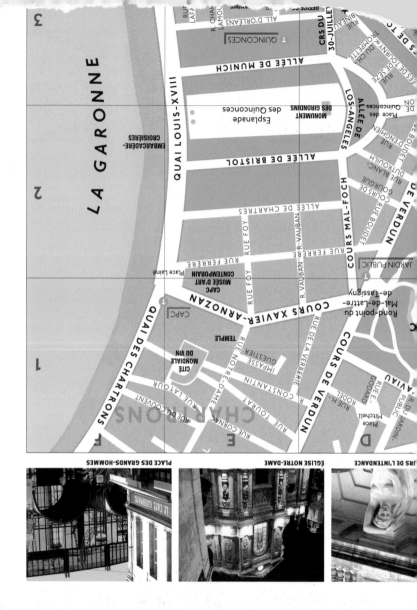

JRS DE L'INTENDANCE

ÉGLISE NOTRE-DAME

PLACE DES GRANDS-HOMMES

LE CAFÉ GOURMAND

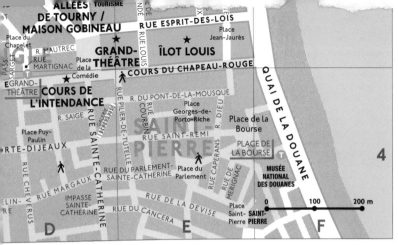

The map labels (top image):
ALLÉES DE TOURNY / MAISON GOBINEAU
RUE ESPRIT-DES-LOIS
Place Jean-Jaurès
GRAND-THÉÂTRE
ÎLOT LOUIS
Place du Chapelet
R. MAUTREC
RUE MARTIGNAC
Place de la Comédie
COURS DU CHAPEAU-ROUGE
GRAND-THÉÂTRE
COURS DE L'INTENDANCE
R. SAIGE
RUE DU PONT-DE-LA-MOUSQUE
Place Georges-de-Porto-Riche
Place de la Bourse
QUAI DE LA DOUANE
Place Puy-Paulin
RUE SAINTE-CATHERINE
RUE SAINT-REMI
SAINT-PIERRE
PLACE DE LA BOURSE
PORTE-DIJEAUX
RUE CHEVERUS
RUE DU PARLEMENT-SAINTE-CATHERINE
Place du Parlement
RUE CAPERANS
RUE DE MÉRIGNAC
MUSÉE NATIONAL DES DOUANES
4
RUE MARGAUX
IMPASSE SAINTE-CATHERINE
RUE DE LA DEVISE
Place Saint-Pierre
SAINT-PIERRE
RELIN-RE
RUE DU CANCERA
0   100   200 m
D   E   F

PALAIS GALLIEN

BASILIQUE ST-SEURIN

...med after Buffon, Diderot, ...ntaigne, Montesquieu, ...usseau and Voltaire, ...ding to the centre of the ...angle. There, in the ...cular square, is a glass ...d iron market-hall where ...u can do your shopping ...d enjoy a simple meal.

Allées de Tourny / ...aison Gobineau (B D3)
...ws of lime trees, classical ...ades, restaurants and ...gh-class shops: since this ...de promenade was laid ...t in 1744, it has come to ...itomise prosperous ...rdeaux. To the north is ...e traffic-filled Tourny ...uare, named after the ...eat *intendant* whose statue ...ominates the square. To ...e south, the Gobineau

House seems to point at the Grand-Théâtre like the prow of a ship. It is the impressive headquarters of the CIVB (Conseil Interprofessionnel duVin de Bordeaux).

★ Jardin public (B C1)
→ *Cours de Verdun*
With its classical French layout, the public garden (1750) was redesigned after the Revolution. The winding river is spanned by little bridges linking the island to the vast lawns of an English-style garden. The shady walks, the calm atmosphere and the botanic garden combine to make this park a favourite afternoon destination for the Bordelais.

★ Muséum d'histoire naturelle (B C1)
→ *5, place Bardineau*
Tel. 05 56 48 26 37; Mon, Wed-Fri 11am–6pm; Sat-Sun 2–6pm
Never mind the creaking floors and draughty windows, this elegant 18th-century house is a treasure-chest of history and learning. Reptiles, mammals, birds, insects, fossils and minerals by the thousand are each painstakingly and meticulously classified.

★ Palais Gallien (B B2)
→ *Rue du Dr-Albert-Barraud*
Over the years, thieves have made off with much of the stone from this ancient 15,000-seat amphitheatre, the only relic of the city of

antiquity (3rd c.). In the Middle Ages, its fine stonework gave rise to the legend of a Carolingian palace, which in turn led to its present name today.

★ Basilique St-Seurin (B A3)
→ *Place des Martyrs-de-la-Résistance; Basilica: Tue-Sat 8.30–11.45am, 2–8pm; Sun noon– 6pm; crypt: daily 2–7pm (June-Sep); Tel. 05 56 24 24 80*
Sculpted Norman porch (11th c.), Gothic chapels (14th–16th c.) and a 20th-century neo-Norman façade for one of the oldest churches in southwest France. The crypt contains tombs from the 4th to the 13th centuries.

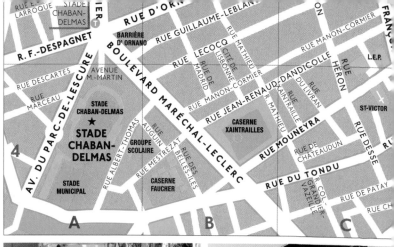

MUSÉE DES ARTS DÉCORATIFS

TRIBUNAL DE GRANDE INSTANCE

★ **Musée d'Aquitaine** (C F3)
→ 20, cours Pasteur
Tel. 05 56 01 51 00
Tue-Sun 11am–6pm
The story of Aquitaine from its origins down the ages, told in a freshly designed setting. Among the fascinating artefacts here (700,000 of them) are Greek vases, a superb Gallic torque (2nd–1st c. BC), a statue of Hercules dug up in the Place St-Pierre (late 2nd c.), a monumental 13th-century rose window and the cenotaph of Montaigne (1593). Upstairs are photographs and videos relating to the recent history of the region.

★ **Cathédrale St-André / Tour Pey-Berland** (C E2)
→ Place Pey-Berland
Tel. 05 56 52 68 10; Tower: daily 10am–6pm (Tue-Sun 10am–noon, 2–5pm Oct-May)
The cathedral is a Gothic masterpiece (13th– 15th c.) with fine statuary and carved spires: only the west front, formerly pushed up against the ramparts, is undecorated. In 1446 archbishop Pey-Berland added a flamboyant campanile, which has a fantastic view from the top. Inside, in the enormous nave (400 ft), is a superb *Deposition from the Cross* by Jordaens (17th c.). In 1137, it was here, before the altar of an earlier church

on the site, that Eleanor of Aquitaine married the French King Louis VII. The subsequent annulment of this union led to 300 years of English domination.

★ **Palais Rohan / Hôtel de ville** (C E2)
→ Place Pey-Berland
The neoclassical palace (1784) of Archbishop Mériadeck, Prince of Rohan, who never lived in it. The façade facing the square is flanked with pilasters and an elegant portico enclosing a fine courtyard. There is a French-style garden at the back, laced with pleasant pathways. Since 1837, the palace has functioned as the city hall.

★ **Centre Jean-Moulin** (C E2)
→ Place Jean-Moulin
Tel. 05 56 79 66 00
Tue-Sun 2–6pm
A war museum dedicate a key hero of the Resista Jean Moulin (1899–1945 founded by his wartime colleague Jacques Chaba Delmas, mayor of Borde from 1947 to 1995. Photc documents, posters and other memorabilia.

★ **Musée des Beaux-Arts** (C E2)
→ 20, cours d'Albret
Tel. 05 56 10 20 56
Wed-Mon 11am–6pm
Two galleries face each other across the garden the city hall. The south w

C

CATHÉDRALE ST-ANDRÉ / TOUR PEY-BERLAND

CENTRE JEAN-MOULIN

MUSÉE D'AQUITAINE

ÉGLISE ST-BRUNO / CIMETIÈRE DE LA CHARTREUSE

Place Gavinies
PASSAGE HERMITE
GAVINIES
R. GÉNÉRAL-DE-LARMIAT
RUE JOSEPH-ABRIA
RUE DE LARMIAT
RUE D'ORNANO
RUE DE LA DEVÈZE
HÔTEL DE POLICE
HÔTEL DE POLICE
RUE C.-DE-ROQUEFEUIL
PATINOIRE
BIB
M.-CRA
RUE
HÔTEL DE RÉGION
RUE COUR
RUE DES SOURDS
RUE DE LESCURE
RUE LEVIEUX
BOULEVARD ANTOINE-GAU
RUE DE DOUMERC
RUE DE CESTAS
R. DES CHÊNES-LIÈGES
CIMETIÈRE DE LA CHARTREUSE
SAINT-BRUNO
HÔTEL DE RÉGION
RUE GEORGES-BONNAC
RUE BLANCHARD-LATOUR
AVENUE D'ARÈS-D'ARÈS
BARRIÈRE
RUE DE LA LIBERTÉ
RUE DE HOURTINS
RUE DE METZ
RUE HANAPPIER
GEORGE
RUE
R. CHAUFFOUR
R. BRIZARD
L'ARMÉE
RUE PIERRE
RUE DE LACANAU
RUE BOUGUEREAU
RUE DE BRACH
R. DESBIEY
RUE DE VINCENNES
IMPASSE FALGERAT
R. SCALIGER
R. BERNARD-ADOUR
PISCINE JUDAÏQUE
Place Duterte
Place Tartas
RUE JUDAÏQUE
RUE JUDAÏQUE
BARRIÈRE JUDAÏQUE
CIMETIÈRE PROTESTANT
RUE E.-LABASSE
AVENUE DE LA RÉPUBLIQUE
BOULEVARD DU PRÉSIDENT-WILSON
R. NAUVILLE
R. CHEVALIER
RUE JEAN-SOULA
RUE DAUZATS
RUE GEORGES-MANDEL
R. J.-FERRY
PETIT
RUE SÉGA
D'ALZON
RUE LACHASSAIGNE
R. DE MARSEILLE
PASS. KIESER
RUE KIESER
RUE DE SOISSONS
R. DE LA BÉNATTE
RUE DE LA PAIX
R. CHARLES-MONSELET
RUE COTREL
RUE PEDRONI
IMPASSE DUCHAUFÉ
ERNEST-DENIS
AV. DU JEU-DE-PAUME
AV. DE MIRANDE
PASS. DE LA PAIX
MANDE
RUE GEOR
RUE C

Pey-Berland / Mériadeck

A gem of Gothic art, the cathedral of St-André stands at the administrative and judicial centre of the city. At its foot, the elegant city hall lines the Place Pey-Berland, always busy with strollers and locals enjoying a cup of coffee in the sunshine. Nearby, the new law courts designed by Richard Rogers seem suspended in mid-air. Also in the neighbourhood are some large museums: the Musée des Beaux-Arts, Musée des Arts décoratifs, and the fascinating Musée d'Aquitaine. To the north, the ever-busy Gambetta square gives on to the Rue de la Porte-Dijeaux, a shopper's paradise, while to the east, the 1970s towers of the Mériadeck quarter continue to excite controversy.

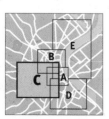

BISTRO DU MUSÉE

CAFÉ FRANÇAIS

RESTAURANTS

Le Palatium (C F3)
→ 164, cours Victor-Hugo
Tel. 05 56 91 47 47
Daily noon–2.30pm,
7.30pm–midnight
Popular with local trades-people, this brasserie is friendly, noisy, and offers good, simple food at unbeatable prices: steak tartare, andouillette, and juicy steaks. €7–15.

Anaël (C E1)
→ 7, rue Judaïque
Tel. 05 56 79 22 50
Mon-Tue, Thu-Sat noon–7pm (9.30pm Fri-Sat)
Walter Deshayes is a gifted chef: not only inventive – he takes inspiration from the four corners of the world, but original – see how dishes are presented. Expect combinations such as tagine of chicken, tataki salmon with coleslaw, spice cake with Szechuan pepper sorbet. Small but carefully chosen wine list. Booking advised.
Carte €10–15.

Scopitone (C E1)
→ 5, rue de la Vieille-Tour
Tel. 05 56 81 75 01; Mon-Sat noon–2pm, 7.30–10.30pm
With rows of tables, benches covered in red leatherette and photos of screen legends on the walls, Scopitone looks like

a Parisian brasserie crossed with a New York diner. Don't miss the duck liver confit (nicer than it sounds) and steaks.
Menu €12; carte €15–25.
Bistro du Musée (C E2)
→ 37, pl. Pey-Berland
Tel. 05 56 52 99 69
Mon-Sat noon–10.30pm
With its bottle-green façade and rows of flagons, this bistro obviously takes its wine very seriously, but with humility. It epitomises Bordeaux, both wine and city, and all with the cathedral of St-André as backdrop. Millefeuille of salmon, cod baked in pastry, and no less than 60 different wines. Set lunch €14.90; carte €15–25.
Bistro du Sommelier (C C2)
→ 163, rue Georges-Bonnac
Tel. 05 56 96 71 78
Mon-Fri noon–2.30pm, 7.30–11pm; Sat 7.30–11pm
At lunchtime this bistro is taken over by workers from Mériadeck; in the evenings it fills up with diners in search of top-notch local cuisine – lampreys, tender entrecôtes, tricandilles, duckling with fruit, and more. Carte €20–35.
Café Français (C E2)
→ 5, pl. Pey-Berland
Tel. 05 56 52 96 69
Mon-Sat noon–10.30pm;

RO DU SOMMELIER

LE RÉGENT

MATIAS MERCAPIDE

Sun noon–3pm
A 100-year-old brasserie which has grown old very gracefully indeed, with velvet seats, ornate moulding, columns and all the traditional trimmings. Outside is a lovely terrace, between the cathedral and the city hall. Try the flank steak with cep mushrooms or the fine plump oysters. Set lunch €18.20; carte €15–35.

Au Bonheur du Palais (C E3)
→ *72, rue Paul-Louis-Lande*
Tel. 05 56 94 38 63
Mon-Sat 8–10pm
Exquisite Cantonese and Szechuan cooking in the 'Palace of Happiness'. The poached crawfish is just short of perfection. Dishes €23.

TEAROOM, CAFÉS

L'Autre Salon de thé (C E2)
→ *11, rue des Remparts*
Tel. 05 56 48 55 43; Tue-Sun 11am–10.30pm (7pm Sun)
Cheesecake, crumble, *tartes* and other utterly delicious pastries are laid on a table in the middle of the room, then served on the finest china, for a tea-time in grand old-fashioned style.

Tearoom of the Musée des Arts Décoratifs (C E2)
→ *39, rue Bouffard*
Tel. 05 56 52 60 49
Mon-Sat noon–6pm
A peaceful courtyard with wrought-iron tables at which to enjoy a well-earned rest after a look at the museum. The brunches are enormous.

Le Régent (C E1)
→ *46, pl. Gambetta*
Tel. 05 56 44 16 20
Daily 8am–12.30am
A long established Bordeaux brasserie, right on the Gambetta square. The perfect spot to sit and watch the world go by.

Les Mots Bleus (C E2)
→ *40, rue Poquelin-Molière*
Tel. 05 56 90 01 93
Tue-Sat 10am–7pm
A literary café, just the place for a cosy chat or to get stuck into that book you brought on holiday. Wide range of coffees, teas, fruit juices and more.

PUBS, MUSIC

Dick Turpin's (C F2)
→ *72, rue du Loup*
Tel. 05 56 48 07 52
Mon-Sat 6pm–2am
A lively small cosmopolitan pub, where you sit and listen to pop, rock and trip hop beneath centuries-old oak beams.

Connemara (C E2)
→ *14-18, cours d'Albret*
Tel. 05 56 52 82 57
Daily 11.30am–2am
Five minutes' walk from Dick Turpin's and the other end of the spectrum: an Irish pub with a giant TV screen, full to bursting point when there's a match on.

Fiacre (C F2)
→ *42, rue de Cheverus*
Tel. 06 63 64 56 62; Concerts 10pm; www.le-fiacre.com
A cellar bar full of memories from the 1980s, when rock was holding out here against the new wave. Now reopened under a new team, it is drawing back the fans of that musical era. Concert €3.

SHOPPING

Pétrusse (C E2)
→ *41, rue des Remparts*
Tel. 05 56 48 21 48
Mon 2–7pm; Tue-Sat 10.30am–1pm, 2–7pm
A stylish cashmere boutique with lilac shawls, saffron scarves, and all kinds of accessories in subtle shades of colour.

Axsum (C E1)
→ *24, rue de Grassi*
Tel. 05 56 01 18 69
Mon-Sat 10am–7pm
A bare, minimalist boutique, stocking all the latest designs for women by Rick Owens, Ann Demeulemeester, Y's Yohji Yamamoto and others.

Matias Mercapide (C D1)
→ *18, pl. des Martyrs-de-la-Résistance; Tel. 05 56 01 45 45*
Mon-Sat 9am–7.30pm
Ostrich, calf or lizard-skin handbags made to order by a talented Argentinian, who used to work for Yves St-Laurent and Hermès, and has his workshop at the back of the shop. Chic but affordable.

Caves St-Genès (C E4)
→ *8 bis, rue Edmond-Costedoat; Tel. 05 56 91 31 81*
Tue-Sat 9am–12.45pm, 4–7.45pm
The herbs and spices on sale in this cellar combine to form a glorious aroma and will transform a simple dish into a work of culinary art. Olive oils from Spain, Italy and Greece, vanilla from Tahiti and New Guinea, fragrant lemon vinegars, and more; 300 wines.

And don't forget...
Galeries Lafayette (C F1)
→ *11, rue Ste-Catherine*
Mon-Sat 9.30am–8pm
Centre Mériadeck (C D1)
→ *Rue du Château-d'Eau*
Mon-Sat 10am–8pm
A shopping centre with some 73 stores.

MUSÉE DES BEAUX-ARTS

PALAIS ROHAN / HÔTEL DE VILLE

Map labels: PASSAGE NICOT · LA LIBÉRATION · RUE LIGIER · RUE DE SAINTONGE · COUVENT DE L'ANNONCIADE · BOURSE DU TRAVAIL · Place de Pressense · R. SAINCRIC · RUE HENRI-IV · Place Sarrail · PORTE D'AQUITAINE · R. SAINTE-CATHERINE · DOUNEYRA · CITÉ MOUNEYRA · COURS ARISTIDE-BRIAND · RUE E.-COSTEDOAT · IMPASSE SAINTE-URSULE · RUE DU TONDU · RUE LOUIS-MIE · RUE DE NAVARRE · RUE DES GANTS · RUE VILLEDIEU · VICTOIRE · Place de la Victoire · R. STE-CÉCILE · R. THÉODORE-DUCOS · R. DE STRASBOURG · Place A.-Larrieu · IMPASSE BOUSCATIER · IMPASSE VIDEAU · RUE MILLIÈRE · RUE LEBERTHON · RUE DONISSAN · R. SAUTEYRON · COURS DE L'ARGONNE · COURS DE LA SOMME · R. DE LANDIRAS · RUE DE PESSAC · R. DE PESSAC · RUE DU PAVILLON · IMPASSE SUCCURSALE · R. CLÉMENT · R. CLÉMENT · RUE MERCIÈRE · RUE PIERRE · RUE DAUDENGE · RUE SAINT-GENÈS · RUE MAZARIN · R. CADROIN · SAINT-NICOLAS · LYCÉE FR.-MAGENDIE · RUE DUHEM · 0 100 200 m · D · E · F · 4

PALAIS DE JUSTICE

ÉGLISE ST-BRUNO

STADE CHABAN-DELMAS

presents the European ⌐hool of the 16th to the ⌐th centuries (Titian, ⌐bens, Chardin and the ⌐rdelais artist Pierre ⌐cour); in the north wing ⌐th and 20th centuries ⌐orks are exhibited, and ⌐clude paintings by Corot, ⌐lacroix, Dufy, Alechinsky, ⌐casso, Kokoschka and a ⌐w local painters, such as ⌐arquet and Lhote.

Musée des Arts ⌐écoratifs (C E2)
→ 39, rue Bouffard
⌐l. 05 56 10 14 00
⌐ed–Mon 2–6pm
⌐e Golden Age of ⌐ordeaux, and the splendid ⌐estyle of its privileged ⌐bility are on display in the

elegant Hôtel Lalande (1779). Magnificent salons and antechambers filled with beautiful mahogany furniture, ceramics, and artefacts in gold, silver and ivory testify to the immense prosperity of the 18th and 19th centuries. Meanwhile, an interesting exhibition of design has been on display on the top floor since 1970.

★ **Tribunal de Grande Instance (C** E2)
→ Rue des Frères-Bonie
The Court of First Instance is housed in seven timber-clad shells supported by a steel and glass construction. Bordeaux, a city of ancient monuments, has been home to this large and

unwieldy UFO, designed by Richard Rogers, since 1998.

★ **Palais de justice (C** E3)
→ Place de la République
Twelve massive Doric columns support the central part of the impressive Law Courts building designed by Adolphe Thiac in neoclassical style and completed in 1846. Crowned by three pediments, it also has two projecting wings on either side.

★ **Église St-Bruno / Cimetière de la Chartreuse (C** C2)
→ Rue François-de-Sourdis
Tel. 05 56 96 41 08 (church)
Amazingly the Revolution spared the extravagant decor of this 17th-century

baroque church: its choir-stalls, an *Assumption* (1673) by Philippe de Champaigne, and an *Annunciation* sculpted by the father of Bernini. At the foot of the church the 60 acres of the Chartreuse cemetery contain some beautiful funerary carvings, while the Catherineau mausoleum has a terrifying allegory of Death.

★ **Stade Chaban-Delmas (C** A4)
→ Bd du Maréchal-Leclerc
Tel. 0892 68 34 33 (box office)
A concrete football stadium (1938) in Art Deco style, home to the Girondins, whose walls shake with the cries of their supporters at every home match.

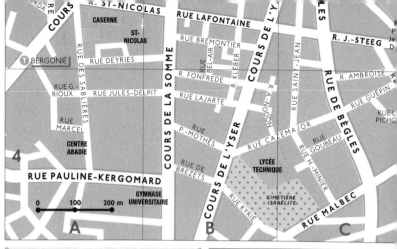

R. ST-NICOLAS
RUE LAFONTAINE
CASERNE
ST-NICOLAS
BERGONIÉ
RUE DEYRIES
RUE BRÉMONTIER
R. J.-STEEG
COURS DE L'Y...
ES
R. AMBROISE
RUE BEL-AIR
RUE KLÉBER
COURS DE LY
RUE SAINT-JEAN
RUE DE BÈGLES
RUE G.-RIOUX
RUE JULES-DELPIT
R. FONFRÈDE
RUE GUÉPIN
RUE LAJARTE
A-NODON
RUE LE PICHO...
RUE MARCEL
RUE P-MOTHÈS
RUE CAZEMAJOR
RUE GOUBEAU
CENTRE ABADIE
RUE DE BRÉZETS
LYCÉE TECHNIQUE
RUE H.-MINIER
RUE PAULINE-KERGOMARD
CIMETIÈRE ISRAÉLITE
GYMNASE UNIVERSITAIRE
RUE KYRIE
RUE MALBEC
0   100   200 m
COURS DE L'YSER
COURS DE LA SOMME

A   B   C

BOURSE DU TRAVAIL

PLACE DE LA VICTOIRE

★ Porte de Bourgogne (D C1)
→ Place Bir-Hakeim
The entrance gate to the old city (1755) looks like the Arc de Triomphe in Paris, and links the Pierre Bridge with Cours Victor-Hugo. Named after the son of the Dauphin (the Duc de Bourgogne), this gate is also known by its other name, the Porte des Salinières.

★ Quartier St-Michel/ Marché St-Michel (D C1)
→ Place Canteloup
Mon am (flea market); Sat am (flea market and food); Tue-Fri, Sun am (antiques)
The St-Michel district has been home to many immigrant Spanish, Portuguese, Africans, Maghrebs and Turks since the 19th century, and the air is filled with the scent of exotic spices. Street names still show the occupations that were practised here: Rue des Faures was home to the blacksmiths, Rue Carpenteyre, to carpenters, and so on. Now the district is popular with the better-off bohemian set, who have moved in and can be seen happily foraging for bargains in the St-Michel market.

★ Basilique St-Michel (D D1)
→ Place Canteloup
Tel. 05 56 94 30 50
Daily 9am–6pm; tower: June-Sep: daily 2–7pm
Now listed as a World Heritage Site by UNESCO, this Gothic masterpiece (14th–16th c.) also boasts the highest tower in southwest France (350 ft). Don't miss the north door (Sacrifice of Abraham, 16th c.), the chapel of St-Sépulcre (Deposition from the Cross, 15th c.), the sculpture of Saint Ursula and the Virgins, (15th c.) and the contemporary stained glass (1960–70).

★ Lycée Montaigne (D B1)
→ 112-124, cours Victor-Hugo
Located on Cours Victor-Hugo, the school is easily identified by its ornate 17th-century sculpted façade and its elevated 19th-century central pavilion. Founded two centuries earlier, in 1761, the school came under the direction of the Collège de Guyenne, whic Montaigne claimed to be the best in France. In the early 19th century, Napoleon made it the firs imperial lyceum, and its prestige has continued to grow ever since.

★ Couvent de l'Annonciade (D A2)
→ 54, rue Magendie
Tel. 05 57 95 02 02; Mon-Fri 9am–12.30pm, 2–5pm
Though it has been the

D

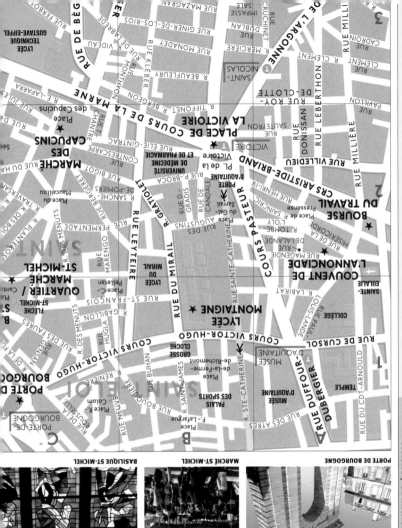

PORTE DE BOURGOGNE

MARCHÉ ST-MICHEL

BASILIQUE ST-MICHEL

Victoire is the time-honoured student quarter of the city, with many of Bordeaux's most popular bars within a stone's throw of the lecture halls. People from all walks of life pass through the square, lending it a cosmopolitan and animated air. To the east, St-Michel has different stories to tell, inhabited by shopkeepers, sailors and immigrants, whose colourful ethnic costumes are visually arresting when set against the austere grey basilica. Further south, Ste-Croix, home of the Beaux-Arts, the National Theatre and the Conservatoire, is the artistic hub of the city, while Saint-Jean, with the central rail station and many nightclubs, remains for now the unfashionable end of town.

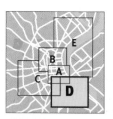

LOS DOS HERMANOS   **CAFÉ DU THÉÂTRE**

RESTAURANTS

Bar-cave de la Monnaie (D D2)
→ *34, rue Porte-de-la-Monnaie; Tel. 05 56 31 12 33 Mon-Sat noon–3pm, 6pm–midnight; closed Sat lunch*
Like its parent restaurant, this lower-priced branch of La Tupina (see below) extols the virtues of high-class local produce in a local-looking setting. Its style may not suit everybody, but diners fond of such traditional specialities as duck confit will have to go a very long way to find a better one at a better price. Dish of the day €9; homemade pâté sandwich €3.

Au Bon Accueil - Chez Fidel (D D2)
→ *12, quai de la Monnaie Tel. 05 56 91 05 26; Mon-Fri noon–2.30pm, 7.30–11pm*
A restaurant serving some of the tenderest beef in Bordeaux to diners made up largely of truck drivers and locals, who watch the news on TV as they eat. Carte €15–30.

Los dos Hermanos (D C1)
→ *52, cours Victor-Hugo Tel. 05 56 91 43 70 Mon-Sat 9am–3pm, 7–11pm*
A very popular Spanish restaurant with a slightly faded and out-of-date

decor, which noone pays attention to anymore. What people come for is on the plate: great anchovies, tortillas, calamari, octopus, Serrano ham etc. Carte €15–30.

Café des Arts (D B1)
→ *138, cours Victor-Hugo Tel. 05 56 91 78 46 Daily noon–midnight*
A historic café-brasserie, beloved of Bordeaux diners from all walks of life who sit contentedly on the cosy red banquettes, scan the list of daily specials and order a carafe of wine before settling down to a fine *entrecôte* with shallots or an *andouillette* (tripe sausage). Packed at mealtimes. Daily menu €11.50; carte €25.

Cochon Volant (D C2)
→ *22, pl. des Capucins Tel. 05 57 59 10 00 Tue-Fri 6pm–4am; Sat-Sun 8am–4am*
The last port of call for many night owls after an evening of exhausting revelry, this former butcher's shop serves delicious *tricandilles*, steaks, sucking pig and other hearty dishes. Carte €25.

Café du Théâtre (D D2)
→ *3, pl. Pierre-Renaudel Tel. 05 57 95 77 20; Tue-Sat noon–2pm, 8–10.30pm*
The exact opposite of the typical Bordelais cellar, it

POMPIER

4 SANS

J.-J. HERRERO

offers contemporary, smart yet welcoming red and black setting. The dishes are overseen by a master in his trade, Jean-Marie Amat, founder of the St-James restaurant and chef at the renowned Prince Noir: the codfish with cockles, milk-fed lamb and squid in ink are all outstanding. In summer, you can eat out on the shady terrace. Satisfaction guaranteed. €30–40.

La Tupina (D D2)
→ 6, rue Porte-de-la-Monnaie; Tel. 05 56 91 56 37
Daily noon–2pm, 7–11pm
A temple to the gastronomy of southwest France, but be prepared for a traditional, rather than typical, image of dining in the region: the setting features baskets of fresh vegetables, birds roasting on spits in the fireplace, and servings of fruit pies just like your mother used to make. Jean-Pierre Xiradakis is also a wizard in the kitchen – though his magic spells have quite a hefty price tag. €40–60.

CAFÉ, BAR, THEATRE

Café Pompier (D D2)
→ 7, pl. Pierre-Renaudel
05 56 91 65 28; Mon-Fri
9.30am–7.30pm (and 9pm–

2am Thu-Sun if events are on) The colourful co-operative café is run by students from the Beaux-Arts, and therefore very lively, with exhibitions, concerts, film shows and other events. Great sandwiches. Membership €2.

Saintex (D B2)
→ 54, cours de la Marne
Tel. 05 56 31 21 04; Thu-Sat & concert nights 10pm–2am
Opened in the wake of the independent record store Total Heaven, Saintex is now renowned for its live music. Decorated throughout in red, it attracts the young set from far and wide to listen to the latest sounds in rock, electro, funk, soul, hip hop and more.

TnBA (D D2)
→ Square Jean-Vauthier
Tel. 05 56 33 36 80
www.tnba.org
The internationally acclaimed National Theater of Bordeaux Aquitaine, renowned for contemporary drama as well as for its productions of familiar classics.

CONCERTS, CLUBS

Comptoir du Jazz (D F3)
→ 58, quai de Paludate
Tel. 05 56 49 15 55
Daily 7pm–2am

Live jazz with touches of blues and funk in a room covered with photos of jazz greats, past and present.

Rock-School Barbey (D D3)
→ 18, cours Barbey
Tel. 05 56 33 66 00
www.rockschool-barbey.com
An unmissable concert venue for music lovers, featuring international names as well as local heroes, mainly from the rock scene.

Son'Art (D B2)
→ 19, rue Tiffonet
Tel. 05 56 31 14 66
Concert nights 8pm–2am;
http://sonartbx.free.fr
Live underground music: rap, electro, drum n bass, rock, folk, world, metal and ska, with occasional exhibitions and live theatre as well.

4 Sans (off D F4)
→ 40, rue d'Armagnac
Tel. 05 56 49 40 05; Fri-Sat & eve of public hols 11pm–4am; www.le4sans.com
A shrine to electronic music located in a huge warehouse: techno, house, Italo-Disco, new wave, booty bass and a whole lot more besides.

L'Hérétic club (D B2)
→ 58, rue du Mirail
Tel. 05 56 92 79 90
www.hereticclub.com

It was once the Zoobizarre, a club catering for the avant-garde, then it was Le Plug, for the techno-rock generation that succeeded it. Now it has become L'Hérétic, an independent anti-conformist venue, where the music is live and the guitar omnipresent.

SHOPPING

Total Heaven (D B2)
→ 6, rue de Candale
Tel. 05 56 31 31 03; Mon 2–7pm; Tue-Sat 11am–7pm
Opened in 1997, this is the best independent record shop in town for reggae, punk, rock and folk music.

J.-J. Herrero (D C3)
→ 3, cours de l'Yser
Tel. 05 56 91 51 96
Mon-Fri 8am–12.30pm, 4–7pm; Sat 8am–12.30pm
Chipirones, mejillones, salt cod and Rioja in a Mediterranean-style deli that is loved by the locals in the Portuguese quarter.

Passage St-Michel (D C1)
→ 14-17, pl. Canteloup
Tel. 05 56 92 14 76
Tue-Sat 9.30am–6.30pm; Sun 8.30am–2pm
Forty antique dealers' stalls on three floors in an old banana-ripening store. Good inexpensive restaurant too.

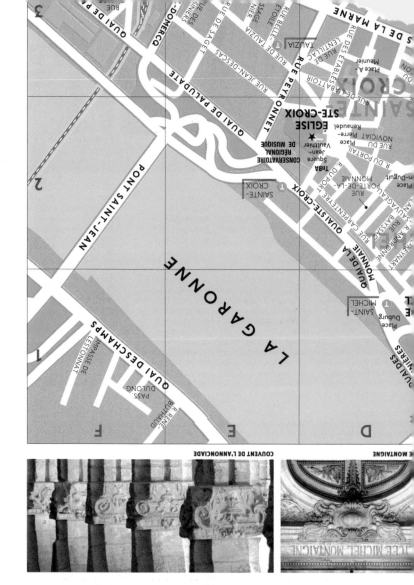

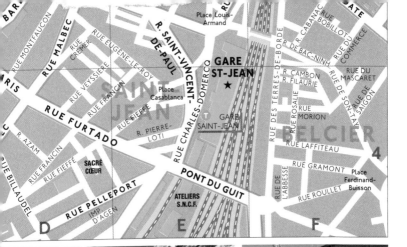

CHÉ DES CAPUCINS

ÉGLISE STE-CROIX

GARE ST-JEAN

d office of the DRAC ⸱artment for regional ⸱ural affairs) since 1995, ⸱old convent has lost ⸱e of its timeless appeal: ⸱fine cloisters are still a ⸱en of peace. Its chapel ⸱o) is in late Gothic style, ⸱the beautiful arcades, ⸱er later in date, ⸱pure Renaissance.

⸱ourse ⸱Travail (D A2)
⸱4, *cours Aristide-Briand*
⸱nmissioned by the
⸱ons in 1938, the 'palace
⸱he people' combines
⸱ austere concrete
⸱struction of the period
⸱ stylish bas-reliefs and
⸱Deco allegorical
⸱scoes.

★ Place de la Victoire (D B2)
Between the campus, the rail station and the city centre, the 'Victoire' is the favourite haunt of students, who crowd its cafés and bars day and night. To the north the monumental Porte d'Aquitaine (1746), decorated with the arms of the city, opens on to the Rue Ste-Catherine. To the east are the steps of the Victor-Segalen medical school with its Third Republic façade. In the centre is a strange red marble and bronze obelisk by Czech sculptor Ivan Theimer, erected in 2005 as a homage to... wine.

★ Marché des Capucins (D C2)
→ *Place des Capucins Market: Tue-Sun 6am–1pm (according to business)*
The old iron-framed hall gave way to concrete in 1958. Five years later the cattle market closed down, and that was the end of the traditional 'stomach of the city'. But the 'Capu' is still there, at least, even if the age of its dominance is over.

★ Église Ste-Croix (D D2)
→ *Place Pierre-Renaudel Tel. 05 56 94 30 50*
An old Benedictine abbey church (11th–12th c.) with a magnificent Romanesque façade that was much

altered in the 19th century, losing the large Gothic rose window but maintaining the medieval character of the building. Inside are some wonderful carved capitals (12th c.) as well as a precious wooden 15th-century figure of Christ.

★ Gare St-Jean (D E4)
→ *Rue Charles-Domercq*
When it opened in 1907, 900 ft long and 110 ft high, the iron hall of the St-Jean railway station was the biggest in the world. Behind its neoclassical façade (1897) in the departure hall is an enormous old map illustrating the main railroad lines in southwest France.

ESPLANADE DES QUINCONCES

CAPC, MUSÉE D'ART
CONTEMPORAIN

★ **Pont de Pierre** (**E** B-C6)
The city's first bridge, commissioned by Napoleon and completed in 1822, was originally a toll bridge until it became the property of the city in 1861. The yellow stone and red brick echo the Palais Gallien (**B**). It is almost 500 yards long and at high tide resembles an embankment with the 17 arches submerged in the River Garonne. At night, its lampposts trace a string of light across the river.

★ **Place
de la Bourse** (**E** A5)
The heart and soul of Bordeaux and its flourishing trade, commissioned by the intendant Claude Boucher

to assert the city's mercantile wealth. The square was built by Jacques Gabriel and his son, Ange Jacques, and then known as the Place Royale (1755). It used many features of the neoclassical style popular at the time: pilasters, columns, grotesque carved masks and, crowning the pediments, allegorical figures: Mercury (trade), Neptune (the waters of the river) and others. At the centre an elegant fountain represents the Three Graces (1864), replacing an earlier statue of Louis XV. In good weather, it is probably at sunrise that the square is revealed in its finest glory.

★ **Esplanade
des Quinconces** (**E** A5)
A neoclassical esplanade laid out on the largest square in France (30 acres), on the site of the former Château Trompette (1453–1816). Beside the river stand two rostral columns (1829) celebrating Navigation and Trade. Higher up are two statues (1858) of Montaigne and Montesquieu in white Carrara marble, while to the west is the monumental column in honour of the Girondins (1899). Liberty stands on top brandishing her chains, while two groups of horses prance in the fountain beneath. Today the square is used for fairs,

circuses and other crowd pleasing events.

★ **Musée national
des Douanes** (**E** B6)
→ 1, pl. de la Bourse
Tel. 05 56 48 82 82
Tue-Sun 10am–6pm
The Customs Museum is located in the Hôtel des Fermes, where the prices all merchandise were once fixed, and tells the story of the oldest official administration in France. You'll see all kinds of devices for detecting fraud and examples of contraband, including confiscated ivory and porcelain. Look out for Claude Monet's superb painting, *La cabane du douanier* (1883).

MUSÉE NATIONAL DES DOUANES

PLACE DE LA BOURSE

PONT DE PIERRE

MUSÉE D'ART

R. VAL DE FERRÈRE

CAPC ★ CAPC

Place Lainé

R. Mal-de-Lattre-de-Tassigny

CRS XAVIER-ARNOZAN

Rd-pt du JARDIN PUBLIC

RUE D'AVIAU

CITÉ MONDIALE DU VIN

TEMPLE

CRS DE VERDUN

Place Mitchell

RUE CONSTANTIN

RUE TOURAT

R. CORNAC

IMP. DU COUVENT

R. NOTRE-DAME

R. SICARD

ÉGLISE ST-LOUIS

RUE DE LA COURSE

RUE DU JARDIN-PUBLIC

RUE DUCAU

QUAI DES CHARTRONS

RUE RAZE

RUE ST-JOSEPH

RUE RAMONET

RUE DE MINVIELLE

IMP. DU

PL. PAUL-DOUMER

PL. PAUL-DOUMER

RUE FRÈRE

RUE PAUL VERLAINE

RUE DUCAU

CRS E.-DE-FAYOLLE

CHARTRONS

QUARTIER DES CHARTRONS 14

RUE DE LA MARTINIQUE

RUE DES BOERS

RUE BASTIE

RUE POMME-D'OR

RUE POMME-D'OR

RUE BARRÈRE

CRS PORTAL

Place Picard

R. CAMILLE-GODARD

N.-D.-DE-LOURDES

RUE CAMILLE-GODARD

Place Paul-Avisseau

RUE POYENNE

RUE DU BEC-D'AMBÈS

RUE D'ARBON

RUE ROSE

COURS BALGUERIE-STUTTENBERG

GOUFFRAND

RUE DU JARDIN-PUBLIC

RUE P.-BERTHELOT

R. DE LA PRAIRIE

RUE MARSAN

COURS DU MÉDOC

ALL. MARTIAL

IMPASSE SAINT-MARTIAL

RUE BINAUD

IMPASSE CONRAD

RUE CONRAD

RUE PRUNIER

RUE MARSAN

Place Saint-Martial

COURS SAINT-LOUIS

COURS JOURNU-AUBER

COURS SAINT-LOUIS

RUE BINAUD

CITÉ CONRAD

RUE ÉMILE-COUNORD

ÉMILE-COUNORD

RUE E.-HUVARD

AVENUE ÉMILE-COUNORD

RUE PRÉMEYNARD

RUE DES FRÈRES-PORTMANN

ALLÉE MARGAUX

COURS DU MÉDOC

COURS JOURNU-AUBER

R. DU BAC

RUE DES FRÈRES-PORTMANN

RUE DE LÉYBL

IMPASSE CABIROLE

Place St-Émilion

COURS SAINT-LOUIS

RUE CHARLES-PLUTO

RUE DU JARDIN-PUBLIC

R HENRI-GUILLEMIN

RUE CHARLES-E.-LÉVÈQUE

ALLÉE DEBORELLE

ALLÉE DEBORELLE

ALLÉE A.-SOUSA-MENDÈS

ALLÉE HAUSSMANN

RACC

COURS LOUIS-FARGUE

GRAND PARC

CITÉ MARSAN

PARC DES EXPOSITIONS ↓

Place Ravésies

PLACE RAVÉSIES

B

A

Recalling the bitter memory of an era whose prosperity was based upon the slave trade, the Place de la Bourse is the finest feature of Louis XV's design for the quays, an imposing ensemble with the Esplanade des Quinconces breaking its continuity to the north. From there the Chartrons district, where the wine merchants used to carry out their business, has found new ways to make a living: the Rue Notre-Dame and the restored quays are witness to a flourishing tourist trade, while the old Sunday market has given way to the chic new warehouses, Les Hangars. Further on are the renovated docks, while the right bank across the river is gradually undergoing its own reconversion.

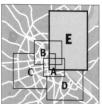

LE BOUCHER

LE SÉLÉNITE

RESTAURANTS

L'Assiette Bordelaise (E B4)
→ 8, quai des Chartrons
Tel. 05 56 52 53 82
Mon-Sat 11.30am–3.30pm
Perfect for lunch in the sunshine, or in the old-fashioned dining room with its tiled floor and ancient posters. Try the *assiette bordelaise* (foie gras, granary bread, Manchego cheese and salad); good hearty fare it is, too. Dishes €8–16.

10 Dowling Street (E A3)
→ 10, rue Sicard
Tel. 05 56 01 20 90; Tue-Sat noon–2.30pm, 7.30–9.30pm
A tearoom doubling as a local restaurant is an odd idea, but a successful one. The owner prepares the dish of the day (excellent pies and duck confit), while his wife brews the tea and minds her small grocery shop, which sells English apples, Marmite, Worcestershire sauce, scones and, of course, baked beans. Pleasant patio, and brunch on Sat. Set menus €12–16.50.

Le Boucher (E B3)
→ 35, rue Borie
Tel. 05 57 87 20 58
Tue-Sun 8pm–midnight
Juicy steaks chargrilled in the fireplace of a tavern

that looks like a country inn, and which doesn't stint on portions either. If a discerning carnivore, this is where you should come for your fix of tender beef. Carte €25–30.

La Petite Gironde (E B4)
→ 75, quai des Queyries
Tel. 05 57 80 33 33; Mon-Fri noon–2.30pm, 8–11pm; Sat 8–11pm; Sun noon–3pm
This restaurant probably has the most attractive terrace in Bordeaux, right by the edge of the Garonne and with splendid views of the quays. Regional, first-class cuisine. Lunch menu €16, carte €30.

Gravelier (E A4)
→ 114, cours de Verdun
Tel. 05 56 48 17 15
Mon-Fri noon–1.30pm, 8–9.45pm
Behind its half-closed shutters is a brightly coloured contemporary dining room with open-plan kitchens, where chef-owner Yves Gravelier adds his personal touch to classic regional dishes, such as the braised red mullet with a coulis of shallots. Stylish and laid back, but rather pleased with itself. Menu €24 (lunch); €26–50.

Le Sélénite (E B3)
→ 6, place Paul-Avisseau
Tel. 05 56 51 05 64; Tue-Sat

E SOUS-MARINE

GASTRONOMIE DES PYRÉNÉES

ANTOINE

noon–2.30pm, 8–10.30pm
Aluminium tables on a
quartz-concrete floor and
plain geometric lines are
the only design in the
wilfully minimalist interior
of La Sélénite. The cuisine
echoes the modernist
spirit of the place: whelks
and green apples with
paprika vinegar, or
duckling with onion
chutney. Love it or hate it,
you'll have to admit it's
got attitude! Lunch menu
€17–22; dinner €30.

Jean Ramet (E A5)
→ 7-8, pl. Jean-Jaurès
Tel. 05 56 44 12 51; Tue-Sat
12.30–2.30pm, 7.30–10pm
A typically French blend
of comfort and elegance
with a clientele to match –
a perfect setting to sample
such gastronomic treats
as hare *à la royale*, or
lobster with vanilla.
Carte €60–70.

CAFÉS, BARS

Café du Musée (E A4)
→ 7, rue Ferrère
Tel. 05 56 44 71 61
Tue-Sun noon–6pm
With its high, brick-vaulted
ceiling, the café of the
Museum of Modern Art is
decorated with works by
Richard Long and furniture
by Andrée Putman. They
do a huge brunch on

Saturdays, either inside or
out on the Japanese-style
terrace.

Chez Alriq (E C4)
→ 2A, quai des Queyries
Tel. 05 56 86 58 49; Tue-Sat
3pm–2am; Sun noon–7pm
(closed Tue-Thu in winter)
With tables scattered
across the grass down
to the river's edge, Chez
Alriq is at its best when
night falls and the quays
opposite light up.
Steaming bowls of
mussels and couscous are
served up, and perhaps
some street theatre on the
side. Different, friendly,
and always busy.

Le Coin rouge (E B3)
→ 53, rue Pomme-d'Or
Tel. 06 62 63 55 76
Tue-Sat 6pm–2am
Before going for dinner
chez Boucher, why not
take an aperitif with the
owner's son in the latter's
peaceful wine bar, with
classical music playing
softly in the background?

L'Avant-Scène (E B3)
→ 36, rue Borie
Tel. 05 57 87 55 88
Tue-Sat 6pm–2am
A piano bar straight out of
a whodunnit, with cool
jazz, billiard tables, and
local characters downing
whiskies at the bar.
Packed to the rafters on
concert nights.

GALERIES, CONCERTS

**Galerie Arrêt
sur l'Image** (E D1)
→ Hangar G2,
Quai Armand-Lalande
Tel. 05 56 69 16 48
Tue-Sat 2.30–6.30pm
Etchings, sculpture and,
through the bay window,
the echoing emptiness of
the wet docks.

Base sous-marine
(off E C1)
→ Bd Alfred-Daney
Tel. 05 56 11 11 50
Tue-Sat 2–6/7pm
Six million cubic feet of
concrete were used by
the Nazis to build this
enormous submarine
base, which is now a huge
arts centre with concerts,
exhibitions and plays.

Satin Doll (E C2)
→ 18, rue Bourbon
Tel. 05 56 50 07 15
Thu-Sat 6.30pm–2am
A great jazz club down a
quiet street, so far known
only to a happy few –
but it's on the up.

CAT (E C2)
→ 24, rue de la Faïencerie
Tel. 05 56 39 87 74
Concert nights 9pm–2am
World music, reggae,
dancehall, grime and
rap at a venue that is
famous for its eclectic
mix of sounds.

SHOPPING

Gastronomie
des Pyrénées (E A3)
→ 12, cours Portal
Tel. 05 56 52 87 59; Tue-Sat
8.30am–1pm, 3.30–7.30pm
A great deli with delicacies
from far beyond the
Pyrenees: lampreys *à la
bordelaise*, foie gras from
the Landes and a thousand
other treats, including rich
Basque cheeses and the
black pork of Bigorre.

RKR Galerie (E A3)
→ 73, rue Notre-Dame
Tel. 05 56 79 35 73
Tue-Sat 10am–1pm, 2–7pm
Designer lighting, smart
table accessories and
stylish furniture are on
display in the street of
antique dealers.

Antoine (E A3)
→ 19-21, cours Portal
Daily 8am–8pm (7pm Sun)
The best patisserie in
Bordeaux, with irresistible
cinnamon buns, *cannelés*,
craquelines, macaroons
and other delights.

Village
Notre-Dame (E A3)
→ 61-67, rue Notre-Dame
Tel. 05 56 52 66 13; Mon-Sat
10am–12.30pm, 2–7pm (and
Sun 2–7pm in Oct-April)
Eighteenth- and 19th-
century antiques in a
gallery housing some
30 dealers.

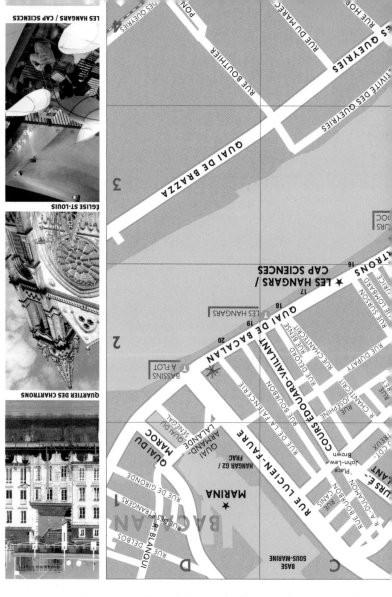

LES HANGARS / CAP SCIENCES

ÉGLISE ST-LOUIS

QUARTIER DES CHARTRONS

RUE HO

RUE DU MAREC

RUE BOUTHIER

PON

DES OUVRIERS

LES QUEYRIES

ACTIVITÉ DES QUEYRIES

QUAI DE BRAZZA

3

DOC
URS

★ LES HANGARS / CAP SCIENCES

16

17 LES HANGARS

18

19

20

QUAI DE BACALAN

2

BASSINS À FLOT

RUE SURSON

RUE DUPATY

RUE CHANTECRIT

R. CHANTECRIT

RUE DELORD

RUE CHANTECRIT

RUE JOSEPHINE

RUE CHANTECRIT

RUE DE LA FAÏENCERIE

RUE LUCIEN-FAURE

COURS ÉDOUARD-VAILLANT

RUE BOURBON

RUE ÉLÉONORE

LOMBARD

RUE BOURBON CANIS

RUE A. DULAMON

R. A. DULAMON

RUE BOURBON

Place
John-Lew-
Brown

QUAI DU MAROC

QUAI DU
LALANDE
ARMANDE / SÉNÉGAL

HANGAR G2 / FRAC

MARINA ★

RUE DE GIRONDE

RUE DES ÉTRANGERS 1

R. BLANQUI

RUE DELBOS

BACALAN

D

C

BASE SOUS-MARINE

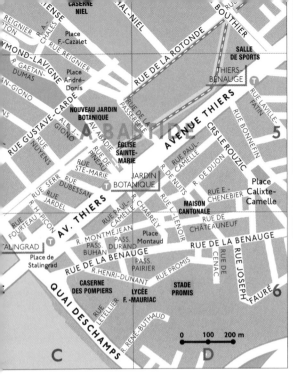

MARINA

RIGHT BANK

**CAPC, Musée d'Art
Contemporain (E** A4)
Entrepôt Lainé, 7, rue
Ferrère; Tel. 05 56 00 81 50
Tue-Sun 11am–6pm (8pm Wed)
The Museum of Modern Art
is located inside the double
nave of a brick warehouse
(1824) formerly used to
store food imported from
the colonies. The important
schools of painting and
sculpture since the 1960s
are displayed in rotation.
There are also temporary
exhibitions out on by the
museum and by the
association Arc-en-Rêve
(architecture and design).

**Quartier
des Chartrons (E** B3)
The historic centre of the
city's wine trade. Originally
marshland, the area was
drained by the Carthusians
(14th c.) before the foreign
merchants arrived. First
came the Flemish, soon
followed by English and
German traders. By the 18th
century, the area was full up:
the beautiful, harmonious
facades of the quays and the
fine, noble houses along the
Cours Xavier-Arnozan date
from this period. In spite of
the decentralisation of trade,
the gleaming glass Cité
Mondiale du Vin (20, quai
des Chartrons) remains a
key centre of business here,
keeping alive the memory
of a little corner of the city
that is still known

throughout the world.
★ Église St-Louis (E A3)
→ 51, rue Notre-Dame
A Catholic church in a
Protestant district (the
neoclassical Protestant
church is at no. 12), built in
1880 and modelled on 13th-
century Gothic cathedrals.
Fine stained glass.
**★ Les Hangars /
Cap Sciences (E** C2)
→ Cap sciences, Quai de
Bacalan Tel. 05 56 01 07 07
Tue-Sun 2-6pm (7pm w/e)
Formerly part of the naval
dockyards, the 19th-century
hangars (warehouses) have
been given a makeover,
with cafés, shops and, at
no. 20, the interactive
exhibitions of Cap Sciences.

★ Marina (E D1)
Bordeaux's marina is
located in a fantastic
industrial setting, and now
with the added attraction of
restaurants, bars and clubs,
which have livened up this
part of the city considerably.
Soon it will also be linked by
a bridge to the right bank.
★ Right bank (E B5)
A new tram link opened up
the right bank bringing a
new breath of life to the now
fast-developing district of La
Bastide. On the Quai des
Queyries are the Botanical
Gardens and a little dancehall, as well as great views
of the left bank. Look out for
the Art Nouveau house at
no. 42, rue de Nuits.

ST-ÉMILION

ABBAYE DE LA SAUVE-MAJEURE

CHÂTEAU DE LA BRÈDE

★ Arcachon (F B3)

→ *Trains leave from Bordeaux St-Jean rail station; tourist office: Tel. 05 57 52 97 97*
A seaside resort with the nostalgic appearance of the Belle Époque, and popular all year round: the Ville d'Hiver (Winter town, 1857), with its opulent villas, once a favourite resort of Napoleon III; the Ville d'Automne, which faces the port; the Ville de Printemps (spring) with its fine Parc des Abatilles near the lively district of Moulleau; and the Ville d'Eté (summer), the heart of the city. The seafront has several small piers, a casino, an aquarium and a whole string of restaurants.

★ Presqu'île du Cap Ferret (F A3)

→ *Buses leave from Bordeaux St-Jean rail station; tourist office: Tel. 05 56 03 94 49*
A narrow sandy beach dotted with pine trees and other flora. The wild coast extends westwards along the ocean. To the east, along the Bassin, brightly painted oyster farmers' huts are scattered from Claouey to the end of Cap Ferret. However today there are fewer fishermen, their place taken by holidaymakers and showbiz celebs. The impressive Dune du Pilat is visible from the end of the peninsula, and to complete a great day

out, make sure to climb to the top of the lighthouse to see the whole peninsula in all its glory.

★ Dune du Pilat (F B4)

→ *Bus from departure point at Arcachon; information (July-Aug): Tel. 05 56 54 63 14*
The highest dune in Europe (347 ft), which changes colour as the day advances, tinted by the Atlantic in the west or the dense pine groves to the east. In the distance is Cap Ferret, which supplies the dune with sand and is always trying to silt up the Bassin.

★ Médoc beaches (F B1)

→ *Buses leave from Bordeaux St-Jean rail station*
There are 50 miles of fine

sand along the Médoc coastline, with several resorts extending from Porge-Océan to the Poin de Grave, though only th surfer's paradise of Laca is at all busy in winter. Out in the estuary stands the fantastic 16th-centur lighthouse, the Phare de Cordouan.

★ Citadelle de Blaye (F D1)

→ *Buses leave from the Bordeaux tourist office; Tel. 05 56 43 68 43 Information: Tel. 05 57 42 12 09*
Built by the military archi Vauban (1685–89), this fortress was only besiege once (1814). Inside its

F

OCÉAN ATLANTIQUE

GIRONDE

D213

MÉDOC

Saint-
Sauveur

Saint-Laurent-
de-Médoc

Listrac-
Méd

Brach

Castelnau-
de-Médoc

D104

D207

D3

D104

Bombannes

Carcans-
Plage

*ÉTANG
DE CARCANS*

Carcans

Maubuisson

Hourtin-
Plage

Port Hourtin

*ÉTANG
D'HOURTIN*

Bourtin-

D4

**BEACHES
★ OF THE MEDOC**
*DE TALARIS
MARAIS*

*FORÊT
COMMUNALE
DE LACANAU*
*ÉTANG DE
COUSSEAU*

Le
Moutchic

Talaris

Lacanau-
Océan

PORT

Lacanau

*ÉTANG
DE
LACANAU*

D6

D5

Sainte-
Hélène

Salaunes

D6

Saumos

D5

D3

Le Temple

D107

D3

Le Porge

D107

Le Porge-
Océan

*FORÊT
COMMUNALE
DU PORGE*

Crohot

Le Grand-

Lège-
Cap-Ferret

*FORÊT
DOMANIALE
DE LIÈGE ET
GARONNE*

Claouey

Ares

Andernos-
les-Bains

Claussat

Lanton

Marcheprime

Audenge

*BASSIN
D'ARCACHON*

*ILE AUX
OISEAUX*

Les Jacquets
Le Piquey
Le Petit Piquey
Le Grand Piquey

L'Herbe
Le Canon

PRESQU'ILE

OCÉAN ATLANTIQUE

D106

D105

D213

D107

D6

OCÉAN ATLANTIQUE

Bordeaux

Blaye

*LAC DE
LACANAU*
*ÉTANG DE
LACANAU*

*ÉTANG
D'HOUTIN*

*ÉTANG DE
CARCANS*

N215

GIRONDE

*POINTE
DE GRAVE*

*PHARE DE
CORDOUAN*

A10

0   15 km

Gironde department

The water and the land of the Gironde department are the soul of Bordeaux. Its soil, rich in clay and gravel and washed by the Garonne and Dordogne rivers, has produced outstanding wines: Margaux, St-Émilion and Sauternes. Today, more and more of its chateaux are open to visitors. But the region has also produced great men: Montesquieu was born at La Brède, while the Bordeaux-born novelist François Mauriac found inspiration in Malagar. Last but not least, the Atlantic has added iodine and salt to its healthy climate: at Arcachon, in the 19th century, the concept of seaside holidays was born. Villas and fishermen's cabins were soon dotted along the coast as far as Cap Ferret.

F

A-B-C
D-E

L'ESQUIREY

CAFÉ LAVINAL

RESTAURANTS

Entre-Deux-Mers
Café de l'Espérance (F E3)
→ 10, rue de l'Esplanade, Bouliac; Tel. 05 56 20 52 16
Daily noon–2.30pm, 8–10pm
A delightful grill-restaurant, with tender entrecôtes, veal steaks or andouillette, served outside in the sunshine in fine weather. Daily menu €15; carte €25.

Bassin d'Arcachon
Le Chipiron (F B3)
→ 69, bd du Gal-Chanzy, Arcachon; Tel. 05 57 52 06 33
Mon-Tue noon–2pm (7–10.30pm summer); Thu-Sun noon–2pm, 7–10.30pm
A short stroll from the fishing port is a local bistro with a strong Spanish emphasis, serving tapas, fish dishes and squid à la plancha. Carte €15–25.

L'Esquirey (F B3)
→ 9, av. du Commandant-Allègre, Andernos-les-Bains
Tel. 05 56 82 22 15; Wed-Sun noon–2pm, 7.30–10.30pm
Feast on whelks, oysters or grilled monkfish in a rustic fisherman's cabin. Don't miss the tiramisù for dessert. Carte €25–30.

Chez Hortense (F A3)
→ Av. du Sémaphore, Le Cap-Ferret
Tel. 05 56 60 62 56
July-Aug: Wed-Mon 7–10.30pm; April-June, Sep: Sat-Sun 7–10.30pm
The mussels at Chez Hortense are famous far and wide. Good food and rustic simplicity, but at a price. Carte €30–50.

Médoc
Guinguette du bout de l'Île (F D2)
→ Chemin du Bord-de-l'Eau, Macau; Tel. 06 13 36 20 41
May-Sep: daily 11am–10pm (Sat-Sun only in April)
A winding road along the estuary leads to this out-of-the-way guinguette (bistro-dance hall). Fillet of red mullet, mussels and great salads. A real find. Dishes €8.50–15.

Café Lavinal (F D1)
→ Place Desquet, Bages, Pauillac; Tel. 05 57 75 00 09
Daily noon–2.30pm, 7.30–10pm
A Franco-Italian-Argentinian menu, where dishes such as bife de chorizo with chimichurri sauce and grilled polenta go surprisingly well with excellent Médoc wine. Daily menu €13.50; carte €25–30.

Cordeillan-Bages (F D1)
→ Bages, Pauillac
Tel. 05 56 59 24 24; Wed-Fri, Sun 12.30–1.30pm, 7.30–9.30pm; Sat 7.30–9.30pm
Asian-inspired cuisine

ΓEAU D'ARSAC · HAUT BERTINERIE · GRAND CORBIN-DESPAGNE

created by the great Thierry Marx, with flavours that certainly spice up classic French cuisine! Hotel. Menus €90–170.

Blaye, Saint-Émilion

Le Bastion (F D1)
→ 11, av. 144ᵉ-Régiment-d'Infanterie, Blaye
Tel. 05 57 42 14 50; Daily noon–2.30pm, 7–10.30pm (Tue-Sun in May-June; Sat-Sun only in Sep-April)
Galettes and crêpes at the heart of the citadel. Be sure to get there early to secure a table on the attractive terrace. Galette €9–14.

L'Envers du Décor (F F2)
→ 11, rue du Clocher, St-Émilion; Tel. 05 57 74 48 31
Daily noon–2pm, 7–10pm
A restaurant at the foot of the church, with a very pretty patio, and 600-label wine list. The veal kidneys are superb. Carte €25–40.

WINE & CHATEAUX

Planète Bordeaux (F E2)
→ RN 89 (exit 5), Beychac-et-Caillau; Tel. 05 57 97 19 35
Mon-Sat 10am–noon, 2–5.30pm (10am–5.30pm in June-Sep)
Organised by the Maison des Bordeaux et Bordeaux Supérieur, this interactive five-part course explains the mystic journey of wine

from the vineyard all the way to the glass. Tasting, and over 1,000 different bottles at competitive prices.

Sauternes

Château d'Arche (F E4)
→ Sauternes
Tel. 05 56 76 66 55
Heady, sweet and powerful whites. Try the 2003 vintage, rich and aromatic at €27.50. Nine guest rooms.

Pessac-Léognan

La Louvière (F D3)
→ 149, av. de Cadaujac, Léognan
Tel. 05 56 64 75 87
A chateau classé (18th c.), producing fine, robust reds and dry whites with a hint of fruit, like the superb 2004 vintage at €20.75 a bottle.

Médoc

La Winery / Château d'Arsac (F D2)
→ Arsac-en-Médoc
Tel. 05 56 39 04 90
Tue-Sun 11am–7pm
La Winery is all about a no-nonsense approach to wine, with discussions, exhibitions and even concerts, in addition to an original glass-walled restaurant, tasting rooms and a retail outlet. The project is the brainchild of the Château d'Arsac (Cru Bourgeois Supérieur).

Lanessan (F D1)
→ On D2 road, Cussac-Fort-Médoc; Tel. 05 56 58 94 80
Daily 9am–noon, 2–6pm
A Cru Bourgeois Supérieur, with spicy aroma and rich finish, notably in the 2002 vintage (€15.50). There is also a Horse Museum with carriages, harness and fabulous stables.

Château St-Pierre (F D1)
→ St-Julien-Beychevelle
Tel. 05 56 59 08 18
A Quatrième Cru Classé (fourth growth) since 1855, rich and powerful, made by Jean-Louis Triaud, a vintner who is also the president of the Girondins de Bordeaux football team.

Lynch-Bages (F D1)
→ Bages, Pauillac
Tel. 05 56 73 24 00
Daily 9.30am–1pm, 2–6pm (Mon-Fri 9.30am–1pm, 2–5pm in Oct-April)
A prestigious name and a Grand Cru Classé with second wines that won't break the bank: the Haut-Bages-Averous 2001 (€23). Tours of the 19th-century vats and exhibitions of contemporary art.

Premières Côtes de Blaye

Haut Bertinerie (F E1)
→ Cubnezais
Tel. 05 57 68 70 74

A pioneer in the system of appellation, and guaranteed quality. Woody whites with a hint of acacia, and intense reds, reasonably priced: €10.90.

St-Émilion, Fronsac, Pomerol

Château de la Rivière (F E2)
→ La Rivière
Tel. 05 57 55 56 56
A majestic and opulent Renaissance chateau, whose terrace enjoys fine views of the Dordogne. Since 2000, it has enjoyed a series of really remarkable vintages (€13.50 for the 2000). Five luxurious guest rooms.

Gombaude-Guillot (F F2)
→ 2, chemin les Grandes-Vignes, Pomerol
Tel. 05 57 51 17 40
Organically produced wines. The robust and luscious 2001 vintage (€24) is a good example of the outstanding value producers insist upon.

Grand Corbin-Despagne (F F2)
→ On D244 road, St-Émilion
Tel. 05 57 51 08 38
Its rich tannin content makes it perfect for laying down. Released in 2003, the 1998 (€25) is fruity and aromatic, and almost at its peak, while the 1955 (this is no typo) can still wait.

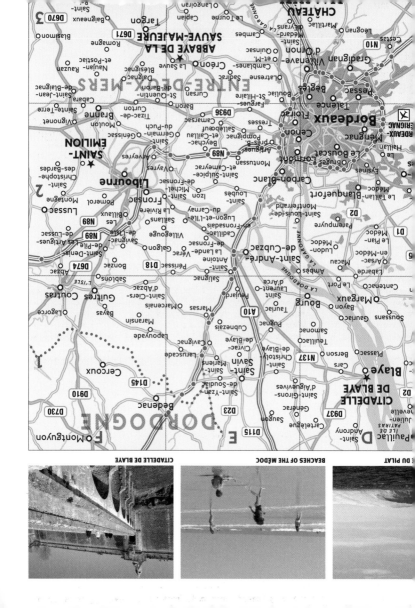

CITADELLE DE BLAYE

BEACHES OF THE MÉDOC

DU PILAT

AGAR / CENTRE FRANÇOIS-MAURIAC

BAZAS

eted walls are an ancient on, a convent and craft ps too. At the foot of its ying ramparts lies the t, silted up estuary of Gironde.

St-Émilion (F F2)
→ *Trains leave from Bordeaux ean rail station;
milion tourist office:
05 57 55 28 28*
ecca for wine-lovers, n two appellations, Premiers Grands Crus ssés, and hundreds of teaux grouped around a dieval stronghold. Its ze of tiny lanes is like open-air museum, and re are lots of exciting ngs to see besides, luding catacombs with

a hermit's cave, and the biggest monolithic church in Europe (9th–12th c.).

★ **Abbaye de la Sauve-Majeure (F** E3)
→ *La Sauve
Tel. 05 56 23 01 55
Daily 10am–6pm (Oct-May: Tue-Sun 10.30am–1pm, 2–5.30pm)*
The vaulted ruins of an 11th-century Benedictine abbey, destroyed first in an earthquake and later by the Revolution. Fine hexagonal tower with viewing platform.

★ **Château de La Brède (F** D3)
→ *La Brède
Tel. 05 56 20 20 49; Late April-May: Sat-Sun 2– 6pm; June-*

Sep: Wed-Mon 2–6pm; Oct-Nov 11: Sat-Sun 2–5.30pm
The chateau of Montesquieu (1689–1755), philosopher and winegrower. The great writer's bedroom and study can still be seen, along with his library of 7,000 books.

★ **Malagar / Centre François-Mauriac (F** F4)
→ *St-Maixant
Tel. 05 57 98 17 16
June-Sep: daily 10am–12.30pm, 2–6pm; Oct-May: Wed-Fri 2–5pm; Sat-Sun 10am–12.30pm, 2–5pm*
The family home of the great writer François Mauriac (1885–1970), with memorabilia, photos, and displays of his life and

work. In summer there are plays, concerts, discussions and dance in the surrounding park which, from its lofty height, was the inspiration for much of what he wrote.

★ **Bazas (F** F4)
→ *Buses leave from Bordeaux St-Jean rail station; Bazas tourist office:
Tel. 05 56 25 25 84*
A little town that is off the beaten track, with a magnificent Gothic cathedral (13th–14th c.) now classified by UNESCO as a World Heritage Site, and a delicious speciality beef known by the jealously guarded name of 'bœuf bazadais'.

TRAIN

St-Jean rail station

The TGV Atlantique links Bordeaux to Paris in 3 hrs (25 trains daily), to Lille in 5 hrs (5–10 direct TGVs), 6 hrs to Lyons (1 TGV), 2 hrs to Toulouse (5–10 TGVs) and 2 ½ hrs to Irun on the Spanish frontier (2–4 TGVs). The Corail train links Bordeaux to Nantes (4 hrs) and Marseilles (6 hrs). The Gironde department is also well served by the local TER train network (Pauillac, Libourne, Langon, Arcachon etc).

Info and reservations
→ *Tel. 3635 (within France)*
www.voyages-sncf.com

TRAM (LINE C)

BOAT

Bateau Ville de Bordeaux (B F2)
→ *Quai Louis-XVIII*
Tel. 05 56 52 88 88
Harbour tours July-Aug: daily 3pm, 4.30pm
Trips round the harbour (a river view of the city) and day cruises on the Garonne and Dordogne rivers and round the estuary.

Péniche (barge) Burdigala (A B2)
→ *Pont de Pierre (right bank); Tel. 06 07 19 75 86*
First Sun of each month
Tour with commentary of Bordeaux's five bridges, along the quays, trips up the two rivers and estuary; also private trips.

CAR

Traffic flow
Easier, now the tram system is complete, but restricted in the Old Town, which will soon be pedestrianised.

Parking
Street parking
→ *24 hrs; €2 per hour; Mériadeck, Bourse, Jean-Jaurès, Salinières, André-Meunier etc*
Public parking lots
→ *24hrs, with charge; Mériadeck, Bourse, Jean-Jaurès, Salinières, André-Meunier*

Fourrière (tow-away)
→ *21, quai du Maroc (E D1)*
Tel. 05 56 50 63 98

TAXI

Taxi ranks in the city centre: expensive.

Allo Bordeaux Taxi
→ *Tel. 05 56 31 61 07*

---

five rooms are beautifully decorated, with parquet floors, marble and fine plaster moulding. Friendly and helpful staff. €75–85.

Hôtel de la Presse (A C1)
→ *6-8, rue de la Porte-Dijeaux; Tel. 05 56 48 53 88*
www.hoteldelapresse.com
Located at the corner of Rue Ste-Catherine and Rue Porte-Dijeaux, the hotel, with nothing but an elevator between the rooms upstairs and the boutiques outside, will go straight to the heart of anyone who loves shopping. Spacious, functional and well equipped, with mini-bar, satellite TV and air conditioning. €74–94.

Hôtel Continental (B C3)
→ *10, rue Montesquieu*
Tel. 05 56 52 66 00
www.hotel-le-continental.com
Located in a quiet street in the Triangle, with rooms decorated in light wood

or, on the upper floors, in pastel shades. The ones overlooking the street are lighter, and those on the top floor look out over the red rooftops of the city. €75–99.

La Maison du Lierre (B C3)
→ *57, rue Huguerie*
Tel. 05 56 51 92 71
Reception: daily 8.30am-noon, 4.30–8pm
Ancient ivy clings to the wall of the pretty courtyard garden where breakfast is served in fine weather. The house belongs to the interior decorator Hélène Devèze, who has transformed it into one of the most attractive places in the city to stay, even if the bedrooms are a little small. €82–95.

Hôtel des Quatre-Sœurs (B D3)
→ *6, cours du 30-Juillet*
Tel. 05 57 81 19 20
http://4soeurs.free.fr

In 1850 Richard Wagner stayed a while here with his mistress, and the romantic view over the Allées de Tourny must have suited the occasion perfectly. Behind a geranium-covered wall are some attractive rooms painted in bright colours or pastel shades. Go for the rooms on the street side. Air conditioning. €85–120.

Une Chambre en Ville (C E2)
→ *35, rue Bouffard*
Tel. 05 56 81 34 53
www.bandb-bx.com
A guesthouse in a street lined with antique shops, and its interior decorated to match, with a lovely curving staircase. The five themed bedrooms reflect the talents of its two owners, who used to run art galleries. Fantastic value for money. €89–99.

AIRPORT

Bordeaux-Mérignac
→ At Mérignac, 9 miles
west of the city centre
Tel. 05 56 34 50 50 / 00
www.bordeaux.aeroport.fr
Links with city center
Jet'Bus
→ Every 45 mins; journey
25–45 mins; €7; stops at
Gambetta and tourist office
→ St-Jean rail station to
airport: daily 6.45am
(7.30am Sat-Sun)–9.45pm
→ Airport to St-Jean rail
station: daily 7.45am
(8.30am Sat-Sun)–10.45pm
Taxi
→ Allo Bordeaux taxi
Tel. 05 56 31 61 07
Journey about 20 mins;
€25–30

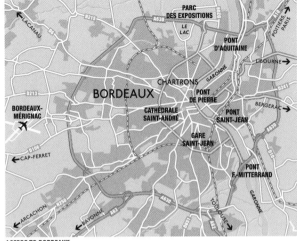

ACCESS TO BORDEAUX

Unless otherwise indicated,
prices given below are for a
double room with en-suite
bathroom in high season
(during school holidays),
but without breakfast.
We recommend you book in
advance.

APARTMENTS
TO RENT

Tourist office (B D3)
→ 12, cours du 30-Juillet
Tel. 05 56 00 66 00
www.tourisme-bordeaux.fr
On the website: six
apartments in city centre
with details of landlords.
Also look in Sud-Ouest daily
paper classified ads.

UNDER €40

Hotel Studio (B C3)
→ 26, rue Huguerie
Tel. 05 56 48 00 14
studio@hotel-bordeaux.com
Forty basic but spotless
rooms, each with its

own TV and shower and at
unbeatable prices. Perfect
for young people on a
slender budget. There are
also two annexes nearby:
the Bristol and Clémenceau
hotels. €25–35.
Hôtel Régina (D E4)
→ 34, rue Charles-Domercq
Tel. 05 56 91 66 07; www.hotel
reginabordeaux.com
Forty no-frills bedrooms,
clean and soundproofed,
in a 19th-century building
opposite the station and
the shuttle stop on the
way to and from the airport.
Inexpensive, and
convenient too. €34–52.

€40–€60

Hôtel Notre-Dame (E A4)
→ 36-38, rue Notre-Dame
Tel. 05 56 52 88 24
www.hotelnotredame.free.fr
Hotels are uncommon in
the Chartrons district. This
one, in the street with all
the antique shops, has

honey-coloured bedrooms,
cable TV and shower or
bath. €47–51.
Acanthe Hôtel (A D1)
→ 12-14, rue St-Remi
Tel. 05 56 81 66 58; www.
acanthe-hotel-bordeaux.com
A friendly welcome with
attractively decorated
bedrooms, each one
different but all carefully
maintained. The street
outside is lined with
restaurants, just off the
Place de la Bourse.
€54–64.
Hôtel de France (B C3)
→ 7, rue Franklin
Tel. 05 56 48 24 11
www.hotel-france-bordeaux.fr
Across from the Jean Vigo
cinema, the Hotel de France
offers remarkably good
value in one of Bordeaux's
more expensive districts.
€55.
Hôtel Gambetta (B C4)
→ 66, rue de la Porte-Dijeaux
Tel. 05 56 51 21 83
Centrally located, only five

minutes from the Triangle,
Gambetta, St-Pierre and the
town hall, this hotel was
completely refurbished in
2007. It is squeaky clean
and very friendly too. €59.

€60–100

**Hôtel de Sèze et Royal
Médoc (B** D3)
→ 5, rue de Sèze
Tel. 05 56 81 72 42
http://hotelsezemedoc.free.fr
Two hotels in one. The Royal
Médoc has 1970s furniture,
which looks a little dated,
while the Hôtel de Sèze,
which also has a slightly
faded air, at least has the
benefit of overlooking the
Allées de Tourny. €60–65.
**Pedroni
Guesthouse (C** B1)
→ 22, rue Pedroni
Tel. 05 56 44 32 36
www.pedroniguesthouse.com
A guesthouse in a 19th-
century building, away from
the noisy city centre. The

Transport and hotels in Bordeaux

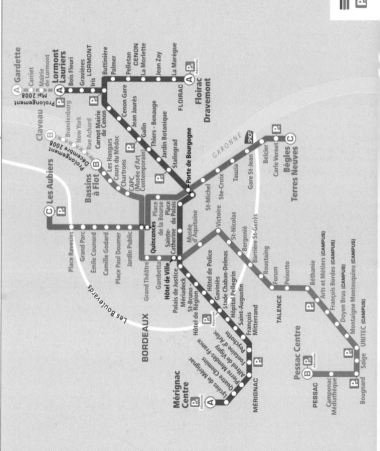

Tramway network

P Parking lots

© latitude-cartagène février 2008

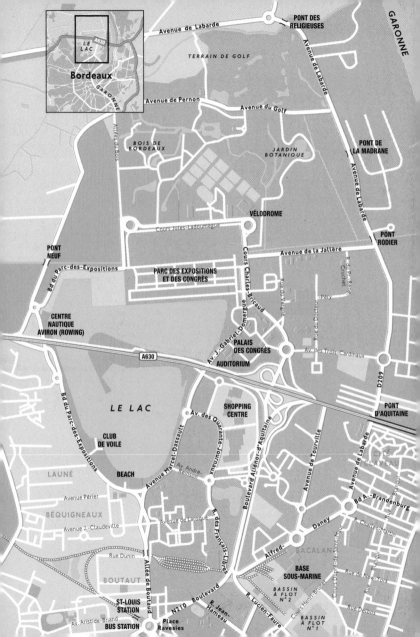

CYCLING PATHS IN THE GIRONDE DEPARTMENT

Legend:
1. Médoc
2. Blaye-Étauliers
3. Bordeaux-Lacanau
4. Arcachon Basin
5. Mios-Bazas
6. Roger-Lapébie

THE WINE ROUTE

CRUISE DEPARTURE POINT

PUBLIC TRANSPORT

Tram and buses of the CUB (TBC) – Réseau Connex
→ www.infotbc.com
Tel. 05 57 57 88 88
Connex runs the bus and tramway systems.

Espace Quinconces
→ Pavillon des Quinconces, Cours du 30-Juillet
Mon-Fri 7am-7.30pm; Sat 9am-7pm

Bus
→ Daily 5am-9.30pm
96 lines serving the whole city network, each connected to at least one tram route.

Evening buses
→ Daily 9.30pm-12.30am
On the 12 main bus routes.

Tram
→ Daily 5am-midnight (1am Thu-Sat)
Three routes:
Line A:
Mérignac–right bank, via Mériadeck
Line B:
Pessac–Marina (to Claveau from Dec 2008), via La Victoire
Line C:
Bègles–Les Aubiers

Tarifs
→ Tickarte: €1.30; valid for one hour on buses and trams
→ Book of ten tickets: €10
→ 'Découverte' ticket (runabout) one day: €4.10
→ 'Découverte' three days: €9.20

Electric trolleycar ('navette')
→ Victoire–Quinconces
Mon-Sat, every 15 mins
It crosses the historic city centre following a blue line marked on the ground. It will only stop if you press the bell.

brasserie, l'Europe, 4,300 square feet of luxury boutiques, a bar, beautiful pool and spa. From €390.

GIRONDE

Hôtel de la Plage (F B3)
→ 1, av. des Marins, L'Herbe, Lège-Cap-Ferret
Tel. 05 56 60 50 15
The century-old little hotel is best known for its restaurant, Chez Magne, which is famed for miles around for its terrific menu – don't miss the fricassee of sepia with saffron – and the moods of its owner; book ahead and eat on the terrace in good weather. Plain bedrooms upstairs with shared showers, overlooking the Arcachon basin and the village – pure bliss. €50.

La Pergola (F B3)
→ 40, cours Lamarque-de-Plaisance, Arcachon
Tel. 05 56 83 07 89

Quiet, well-maintained bedrooms, offering some of the best value to be had in the Ville d'Été (summer town). €70–91.

Château du Petit-Puch (F F2)
→ Saint-Germain-du-Puch
Tel. 05 57 24 52 36
www.chateaupetitpuch.com
Four attractive guestrooms in a 14th-century winegrowing château near St-Émilion. Breakfast is served in the garden or in an ancient vaulted chamber. €80.

Hôtel de la Citadelle (F D1)
→ Place d'Armes, Blaye
Tel. 05 57 42 17 10
www.hotellacitadelle.com
The only hotel in the citadel, equipped with every convenience (satellite TV, pool, garden, air conditioning) and with spectacular views of the estuary in the distance. €80.

Le Relais de Franc-Mayne (F F2)
→ 14, La Gomerie, St-Émilion
Tel. 05 57 24 62 61
www.relaisfrancmayne.com
The six luxurious bedrooms of the Château Franc-Mayne (Grand Cru Classé) make for an intriguing mixture of styles, such as 'British Landscape', 'Indian Fusion', 'Pop Art', and others. €160–230.

St-James (F E3)
→ 3, pl. Camille-Hostein, Bouliac; Tel. 05 57 97 06 00
www.saintjames-bouliac.com
A grand glass and timber construction designed by Jean Nouvel, inspired by a tobacco-drying shed and standing in its own verdant grounds. A satisfying blend of nature, light and voluptuous luxury. The restaurant too is superb, under the masterly direction of Michel Portos. €210–430.

BORDEAUX ST-JEAN RAIL STATION

CYCLING

With 300 miles of cycle paths and 1,300 miles of marked tracks the Gironde department has one of the best networks of this kind in the country.

Six paths:
Médoc: along the coast
Blaye–Étauliers: riverside paths around Blaye
Bordeaux–Lacanau: from the city to the surfers' paradise
Arcachon Basin: around the basin and back to Bordeaux
Mios–Bazas: from the Arcachon Basin to Bazas
Roger-Lapébie: in the Entre-Deux-Mers region.

Hôtel de Normandie (B D3)

→ 7-9, cours du 30-Juillet
Tel. 05 56 52 16 80
www.hotel- de-normandie-bordeaux.com
One hundred comfortable rooms of various sizes in a hotel that dates back to 1903. From the windows all you see is the Quinconces esplanade, with a view that goes right down to the river. €93–230.

€100 AND OVER

La Tour Intendance (C E1)

→ 16, rue de la Vieille-Tour
Tel. 05 56 44 56 56
www.hotel-tour-intendance.com
Silky sheets to help you drift off to sleep in a beautiful old-world hotel with solid stone walls. A step back in time, and one of the most comfortable places to stay in the city

centre. TV and air conditioning. €118–148.

Hôtel Bayonne Etche-Ona (B D4)

→ 15, cours de l'Intendance (entrances: 4, rue Martignac and 12, rue Mautrec)
Tel. 05 56 48 00 88
www.bordeaux-hotel.com
Two 18th-century houses and two hotels, the Bayonne and the Etche Ona, now linked under the same banner. Comfortable, well decorated rooms, if a bit overdone. The fine 17th-century Basque furniture in the Etche-Ona puts it a notch above its partner. €159–285.

Petit Hôtel Labottière (B B1)

→ 14, rue Francis-Martin
Tel. 05 56 48 44 10
The two splendid apartments of this sumptuous 18th-century townhouse (now a listed historic monument) are miniature museums. The

friendly owners will tell you everything there is to know about their house, and their city. The breakfast served here is out of this world. €180.

Hôtel Seekoo (E C2)

→ 54, quai de Bacalan
Tel. 05 56 39 07 07
www.seekoo-hotel.com
An iceberg (seekoo in Inuit) in a fast changing area of Bordeaux. This gleaming white modern structure has a comfortable, luminous white minimalist interior and state-of-the-art lighting. Highly original (some beds are round, some wash basins free standing) and luxurious too, complete with Turkish bath and bar. €180–360.

La Maison Bord'Eaux (B A2)

→ 113, rue du Dr-Albert-Barraud; Tel. 05 56 44 00 45
www.lamaisonbordeaux.com
Behind the entrance to a fine old town house

stands a fantastic piece of contemporary interior decoration, the work of designer Brigitte Lurton (who is also a relative of some famous winegrowers). Its pure lines and muted colors make it impossible not to feel at ease in this beautiful hotel complete with library, wine bar, garden and six elegant bedrooms located in a quiet street away from the city noise. €180–230 (breakfast included).

Hôtel Regent Bordeaux (B D3)

→ 2-5, pl. de la Comédie
Tel. 05 57 30 44 44
www.theregentbordeaux.com
Opposite the Grand Théâtre stands Bordeaux's newest deluxe hotel, opened in 2008 and remodeled in the grand style by the French designer Jacques Garcia. With a gastronomic restaurant, L'Océan, a

Street names, monuments and places to visit are listed alphabetically. They are followed by a map reference of which the initial letter in bold (A, B, C...) relates to the district and matching map.